MY HORSE, MY PARTNER

MY *Horse,*
MY PARTNER

Teamwork on the Ground

LISA WYSOCKY

THE LYONS PRESS
Guilford, Connecticut
AN IMPRINT OF THE GLOBE PEQUOT PRESS

To buy books in quantity for corporate use
or incentives, call **(800) 962–0973**
or e-mail **premiums@GlobePequot.com**.

The Lyons Press is an imprint of The Globe Pequot Press.

10 9 8 7 6 5 4 3 2 1

Printed in the United States of America

Designed by Claire Zoghb

Library of Congress Cataloging-in-Publication Data

Wysocky, Lisa, 1957–
   My horse, my partner : teamwork on the ground / Lisa Wysocky.
       p. cm.
   ISBN 978-1-59921-123-7
   1. Horses—Training. 2. Horsemanship. I. Title.
   SF287.W97 2007
   636.1'0835—dc22

                                                2007011224

THANK YOU

to all my equine partners, including

Dondi, Snoqualmie, and Ben;

and to therapeutic riding horses

everywhere.

CONTENTS

ACKNOWLEDGMENTS

My Horse, My Partner would not be a reality if it were not for the efforts of all of the following, each of whom played a part in bringing this book to you. My friend and agent, Sharlene Martin at Martin Literary Management, who admittedly knows nothing about horses, introduced me to the great people at The Lyons Press and was the catalyst for bringing the book to fruition. Thank you, Sharlene! I have enjoyed meeting and working with the people at The Lyons Press, including Eugene Brissie, Kathryn Mennone, Jessie Shiers, and Maureen Graney, and am very proud to be part of their stable of authors.

I am very fortunate to be able to train horses at Saddle Up!, a riding program for children with disabilities in Franklin, Tennessee. They graciously allowed me free rein of their horses and beautiful state-of-the-art facilities for this book, and all the photos you see were taken at this magnificent facility. Thanks also to the Saddle Up! board of directors and staff for allowing me to be part of such a wonderful program. My sincere appreciation goes to the Saddle Up! program riders and volunteers, who never fail to make my day and who have prevented me from turning into a writing recluse. Special thanks to volunteer stable hands Teresa Barry, Jessica Caldwell, Marty Foy, Suzanne Fuller, Jenn Krause, Ann Quigley, and Penny Wilson, who groomed horses, moved equipment, and never complained during a very warm three-day photo shoot, and to Cheryl Dellamedaglia, who made sure my boots were free of manure and that there was no broccoli in my teeth. And my eternal gratitude to Lady, Lucky, Nacho, Nelson, Nomo, and Valentino, six of the Saddle Up! horses who continue to amaze me with their patience and kindness. Even when they fully believe I have lost my senses, they each do their best to excel in whatever is asked of them.

To Altair Brondini, Roy Johnson, Becca Shaffner, Tim Covin, and all the other great people at Nutrena Feeds, thank you for supporting me. To Rick Lamb, thank you for all the book blurbs, event tickets, and promotion. You have no idea how much I appreciate it all. A huge thank you also to Terri Knauer for her continued support.

Thank you to photographer Colby Keegan for making both the horses and me look great, and to Bill Vandiver of The Edge of Belle Meade Salon for taking care of my flyaway hair. Additional thanks to Bruce Uher at MultiMedia Interactive for the great Web site and for shooting the DVD version of *My Horse, My Partner*; to Keith Bartz, Alice Hoff Lear, Jack Brainard, Dick Kisner, Lili Kellogg, and Sue Byers for teaching me far more than just how to ride; and to my mother, Pat Wysocky, for making those lessons possible.

Introduction

Desensitization, trust, confidence, and respect. These are the corner-stones of a healthy experience with horses. I first began developing My Horse, My Partner ground activities when, as an eleven-year-old child, I bought an eighteen-month-old pony for forty dollars. As he was too young to ride, I "invented" things to do with him, based on what I could learn from the meager stock of equestrian books in our local library. Before too long, Dondi was wearing an elaborate rope harness covered with pots and pans, paper bags, and any childhood toy I could find that would either blow in the wind or make noise.

Dondi and I were soon walking up and down the streets of our suburban neighborhood, he dressed as creatively as possible, and I making sure he was leading properly, with his ears next to my shoulder. The neighborhood walks gave way to longeing sessions in our backyard, and later in the pasture of a friend's house after we moved Dondi to larger quarters.

The longeing led to long-line sessions in which Dondi learned to turn and stop, and those progressed to actual driving sessions in which Dondi pulled a "travois"—two long poles, one attached to each side of his baling-twine harness, with a 2x4 nailed to the other end of the poles. I eventually strung the poles with every noisy, blowy thing I could find and drove him around the pasture and up and down a nearby gravel road.

The upshot of all this was when Dondi was old enough to ride, he was a steady, unflappable pony who only needed to learn seat and leg aids. It was many years before I realized it, but through Dondi, the foundation for My Horse, My Partner desensitization and ground training activities was complete.

○○

I often compare a herd of horses to a classroom of second graders. In a five-minute period, both can run the gamut of emotions and behaviors: from exuberance to sadness, poutiness to playfulness, studiousness to practical joking. And, as with second graders, horses have to be taught that there are appropriate moments for each. It's okay to nip

My pony, Dondi, and I both became well acquainted with pom-poms at an early age.

and run and kick with your equine buddies, but not with your human partner. You can be playful and buck and spook amongst the falling leaves in the pasture, but not on a trail ride with your human friend.

Kids and horses also have fight-or-flight mechanisms, instinctive reactions to real or perceived threats for which each has to learn the difference. While the nature of a child will determine whether they fight or run away, horses, for the most part, instinctively flee from objects and situations that look threatening. The key is that virtually anything can look threatening to a horse if they have not seen the object—or something similar to it—before.

I once had a three-year-old gelding who was so terrified of white plastic bags that he broke one of the barn's support beams in three pieces. He had been tied with a breakaway clasp that for some reason did not break away when he caught sight of a white plastic garment bag draped over a feed bin. He then crashed through a wooden barn door, reducing it to splinters, bucked through a three-board fence into the neighbor's paddock, sprinted across their land, leaped over the fence on the other side, and finally came to a trembling halt in an alfalfa field a quarter mile away.

This situation, obviously, was both dangerous and expensive. Neighbors tend to become unfriendly when your horse destroys fencing and presents escape opportunities for their herd. When barn owners have to replace support beams, doors, and fences, they sometimes raise boarding fees. But most importantly, when horses become so fearful that they act in a dangerous manner, people can get hurt. I was fortunate that both the neighbor and the owner of the barn took it all in good stride, and also that I did not get hurt during the horse's frantic attempt to put great distance between himself and the "killer" garment bag. But the situation could easily have turned out very differently on all accounts.

It was sudden, unpredictable situations such as these that made me remember Dondi, and I began including desensitization training and ground exercises with every horse I had in my show barn. It didn't matter if the horse was a twelve-year-old multinational champion youth or pleasure horse, or a yearling halter phenomenon. They all had My Horse, My Partner training, as did my student riders. The result was confident, capable riders who could work with their horse to learn new skills. These were riders who analyzed problems as they developed and discovered creative solutions on their own. Rather than calling me every five minutes to ask how to deal with a new situation, my students developed an instinctive response that invariably gave them the correct answer.

The horses were also some of most unflappable on the show circuit. I remember trimming the hair on a yearling halter gelding's ears in the barn aisle at a horse show as my barn crew cleaned stalls and moved bales of hay and shavings behind him. Not only was the horse not cross-tied, he wasn't even wearing a halter. Other trainers were amazed that I had no qualms that this young horse would fuss or move, but he had been through many of the desensitization and ground training activities and trusted me as much as I trusted him. In hindsight, the horse should have been haltered as a safety precaution, but I so trusted the horse that at the time I felt it was not necessary.

As I went through my competitive career, I found ways to teach my desensitization and ground training activities not only to my students, but also to many of the owners of the horses I trained. Most did well because the concepts are simple; this is not rocket science. Instead, this method of desensitization and ground training is a slow, methodical process that anyone with a little horse sense can employ with good results. In the end, both horse and human build respect, confidence, and trust in themselves and in each other.

The equine owner or trainer—or as often referred to here, the human partner—need not even know how to ride. My experience has been that there are many equine enthusiasts who, for reasons that include health, injury, or lack of experience or time, do not ride. These ground partners can also be parents who help sons and daughters at the barn or at horse shows; grooms at professional stables; owners of breeding, show, or race horses; barn, stable, or farm managers; and even some trainers and riding instructors who may once have ridden, but due to age or injury no longer do so. But all of the above have frequent interaction with horses on the ground. Understanding desensitization and ground training procedures can help make their experiences safer and more fulfilling as they develop confidence in their own abilities, and respect for and trust in their equine partners.

Of course, many horse people do ride, and the respect, confidence, and trust riders and their horses develop through My Horse, My

Partner ground activities will make their mounted journeys safer and more enjoyable.

Ground and desensitization training can be done at any stage of a horse or human partner's development. And, while the best results come from a quiet, unabused horse who is at least eighteen months old and who has no existing phobias, the vast majority of horses can be helped significantly, regardless of breed, temperament, age, and past experiences. Unfortunately, there are a very few horses who have been so badly traumatized or abused that they are dangerous no matter how you try to help them. These horses are, thankfully, very few in number, and recognizing them will be discussed in Chapter Two.

While I feel every horse should receive My Horse, My Partner ground training (you never know when your horse will encounter her own version of a killer garment bag), horses who will most benefit are young or inexperienced horses, insecure horses who spook easily, horses who do not listen to their human partners, and horses with behavior problems.

I developed these activities for anyone who wants to receive more enjoyment from his or her horse. Growing up, I worked very hard for every saddle—and every brush and curry comb and piece of baling twine—I owned. I realize that not everyone has access to fancy barns or a variety of saddles, so there is no need here for expensive training equipment or huge facilities. A round pen and a training surcingle are helpful to have, but not necessary, as you can usually find and adapt alternatives that are already on hand. Areas that could be used to train instead of or in addition to a round pen might include a stall, paddock, pasture, riding ring or arena, or barn aisle. An old saddle or a couple of Western cinches can be substituted for a surcingle, and most of the other equipment needed can be found at a discount department or thrift store.

While some of the needed skills and techniques will take time for both horse and human to master, most do not require a lengthy period of time every day, for I realize that most people also have other areas of their lives. Job, school, and family obligations all are important and pull at our time.

Saddle Up!, the riding center for children with disabilities where I currently serve as equine trainer, has seen tremendous improvement over a year's time with an older gelding who is obstinate about many things, including walking over poles and going up to a mailbox. How much of his behavior is fear and how much is stubbornness, I do not know. In the long run it does not really matter, as the training method in My Horse, My Partner is the same regardless of the cause. But what I do know is that with one Saddle Up! volunteer working approximately half an hour a week, this horse has made amazing progress. Would he have made more progress if he had been worked with two times a day, five or six days a week? Certainly. But we all do what we can in the time we have. If you have less time, your progress will be no less significant, just slower.

My Horse, My Partner works very well for horses used in equine assisted activities because riders with disabilities may not have the strength or balance to stay mounted if a horse spooks or makes an unexpected movement. Instructors may also use a variety of unusual toys, games, and adaptive equipment to help the rider achieve his or her goals. Consequently, therapy horses have to become used to many different types of sounds and movements. But so do horses who spend time in competition, on the trail, or in your backyard.

Prior to my work in therapeutic riding, I spent many years training Arabian, Morgan, Appaloosa, and Quarter Horses for the show ring. I know from experience that My Horse, My Partner activities work well for all breeds, all ages, and all disciplines. A fifteen-year-old Quarter Horse used in 4-H will accept some ideas more quickly than a three-year-old Arabian who is just starting out—and vice versa. Each horse is unique, and you will learn to go as fast or slow as your horse tells you she is comfortable.

But why spend the time at all? Why go through a lengthy training program, especially if you already have a good relationship with a horse who has no major problems? There are several answers to this.

1. You can never trust your horse enough. No matter how solid you feel she is, she can always be accustomed to more outside stimuli.

2. The process of desensitization and ground training is a learning process that gives the human partner the tools to work with virtually any horse and any problem. Horses, like rabbits, tend to multiply. If you own one horse, chances are that at some point in the future, you will own another, and that other horse may not be so perfectly mannered.

3. Most importantly, this program will allow you to get to know your horse in an entirely new manner. Your horse truly is your partner in many ways, and the better you know each other, the better your equine experience will be.

My youth horse was a little Appaloosa mare who was a member of our family for twenty-three years. Over several decades, we got to know each other very well. When she dropped her head and tipped her nose to the right, I knew she was ready to give up and be caught. I learned that she loved to put her chin on my shoulder and have me rub her cheeks in a circular motion. She'd close her eyes and groan until I had to stop because the weight of her chin was making my shoulder numb. Snoqualmie was also a supportive presence when I was doing tough homework, my books sprawled out on her rump, me sitting backwards on her broad back as she grazed.

Later, I trusted her implicitly with my then four-year-old son when she, my son Colby, and our Shepherd-Labrador dog Dexter played pirates in the pasture. Snoqualmie was the pirate ship and Dexter was the "attacking" pirate. They played for hours, the three of them each wearing elaborate costumes. Snoqualmie loved every minute of this game. Certainly she understood the "rules" far better than I ever did. One of her jobs was to serve as the gangplank, raising and lowering her neck on command as Colby either climbed up to sit on her back, or slid down to make another rush at the opposing "pirate." Snoqualmie would also happily follow "Captain" Colby's directions to move to such strategic locations as under the big tree, or near the pond.

Snoqualmie was my best friend and taught me that a horse can be more than transportation, more than a ticket to a blue ribbon, more than another mouth to feed. Your horse most likely has wonderful personality traits and preferences that you can't yet imagine. *My Horse, My Partner* can help you discover the hidden personality that is your horse. Believe me, that is definitely something you do not want to miss.

Safety is of primary concern with *My Horse, My Partner*. That's why it is very important that both the horse and human partner tackle each step in order, and that no step be started until the one previous to it is completely mastered. As you will see at the end of these activities, your equine partner will be able to carry a number of odd objects—including umbrellas, pom-poms, plastic bags, and pots and pans—without batting an eye. He will be able to withstand unexpected loud noises and pull scary objects. However, if you ask your horse to do any of that without thoroughly mastering the earlier activities, both you and your horse could be hurt. It is also a good idea to read through the entire book before starting. This will give you a better feel for the concept, and for the progress you can expect to make.

If you have several horses, I suggest you choose just one to partner with for these activities. In addition to helping your horse become a safe and trusted companion, you will be exploring this horse's personality and teaching your partner about yourself. After you have fully completed the process, you can then go back and enrich the lives of your other horses and extend your new knowledge to these other equine friends.

Now let's get started.

YOUR TOOLKIT

A little over a year ago I found myself holding my breath in the center of the Tennessee Miller Coliseum on the campus of Middle Tennessee State University as I prepared to longe a then four-year-old Tennessee Walking Horse cross. The horse, Valentino, and I were part of a therapeutic riding demonstration at the Volunteer Horse Fair, Tennessee's annual state horse expo, and there were several thousand people in the audience as I played out the longe line.

The reason I was holding my breath was because this wasn't just any horse, and this wasn't just any longeing session. This was a horse who had been abandoned as a yearling and was left to fend for himself in a small, sparse pasture. When various neighbors remembered, or had the money, they would throw this little dark horse a bale of hay. After a year, Horse Haven of Tennessee, an equine rescue organization in the Knoxville area, stepped in and rescued him. He came to Saddle Up! a few months later, having been fed, wormed, and gelded, and after having had three sessions as a demonstration horse for clinician Craig Cameron at that year's horse fair. At the time of his arrival, Valentino was not really halter broke, did not tie, and due to his prolonged isolation, had no idea how to relate to people, much less other horses.

Why, you ask, would a program that helps children with disabilities be interested in adopting such a project horse? One, at 14.2 hands

Valentino was the perfect size for Saddle Up! program needs. Two, he had incredibly rhythmic and cadenced gaits at the walk and trot, which is very important in therapeutic riding. Three, he was very smart and starved for affection. Saddle Up! was hoping the investment of one year's time would pay off in having this horse in their program for twenty or more years.

So here Valentino and I are a year later in the center of the coliseum ready to show the world how we took this ribby, untrained youngster and turned him into a horse trustworthy enough to carry children with disabilities in less than a year. I say "we" because the effort made with this horse was not just mine, but also that of many Saddle Up! volunteers, some of whom had very little equine experience.

Earlier I said this wasn't just any longeing session. And it was not. It was a demonstration to show how we desensitized Valentino, and got him to trust both himself and us. In addition to a halter and longe line, Valentino was wearing a longeing surcingle with ladder reins attached over his back and under his tail. Ladder reins are a piece of adaptive equipment sometimes used in therapeutic riding. Think of regular English reins with cross pieces, like rungs on a ladder, every six inches or so. (Holding onto one of the cross pieces helps the rider know how long or short to hold the reins.) Then, snapped to the surcingle and ladder reins were sleigh bells, a black plastic bag, rattles, a plastic grocery bag with a pie tin and plastic ball inside, two pom-poms, a plastic milk jug with a few pebbles in it, a vinyl feed bag, and various cloth streamers. To top it off, around his neck he wore a multicolored slinky and between his ears a colorful blue pom-pom. In short, Valentino looked like a junkman's truck and sounded like a one-horse band.

The goal of Valentino's desensitization training had been to accustom him to different groups of objects that encompassed various colors, sounds, and movement. He had been through this training so much at home that this very unique group of objects had become, to him, routine. The training also built much-needed trust in his human partners, and confidence in himself. But with the added stimulation of new surroundings, the echo of the loudspeaker, movement of people in the stands, and the wide open space of the arena, would Valentino remember his training, or would he panic and try to flee? That's why I was holding my breath.

Many of the My Horse, My Partner activities involve building confidence in the human partner. Remembering how important confidence is to a horse, I let out my breath, swallowed my doubt, presented confident body language and facial expressions, and played out the longe line with a firm command of "Valentino, walk on." For the next ten minutes Valentino quietly and confidently walked, trotted, cantered, reversed, and stopped on cue, his head low, his ears flicking in my direction, as I explained the desensitization process to the audience. Then he stood quietly in the corner of the arena with a teenage volunteer for another twenty minutes as other aspects of the Saddle Up! program were demonstrated.

I have been proud of many things in my life, but this little horse is close to the top of the list. He came a long way in a very short time with many inexperienced people working with him. But Valentino's story does not have to be unique. You, too, can progress just as far—or even further—with your equine partner. But before you pull out your longe line and round up your horse, the first step is to line up your toolkit.

The following training tools are only suggestions. You may not have access to all of the items, or you may find substitutions that work better for you. The one important rule is to include items from every category: basics, audio, visual, and movement.

As we go through the list and the My Horse, My Partner activities, you will find that your equine partner may readily accept objects from one, and be hesitant to accept those from another. This is common and has to do with how your individual horse lives in his or her environment. Some horses smell new objects, others taste them, some snort, and a few stare at the new thing for hours at a time. These are the smellers, the tasters, the snorters, and the starers. And, there are a few horses who do all of the above. As we progress, you will see how your horse reacts, and will learn to offer more items that he is uncertain about, and fewer that he readily accepts. You will also learn to predict your horse's reaction to new stimuli in advance and to reassure him in a way that he understands.

THE BASICS

Items in this group include standard horse equipment you probably already have around your barn. Unlike the other categories, you will need most of the items in this group, or something similar. We'll discuss the use of each item as we go through the various activities. For now it is enough to know that you have it on hand, or that you will need to find a substitution.

HALTER

Rope, leather, or nylon—the material the halter is made out of doesn't matter, as long as the halter is in good working condition and fits well. This last part is very important. As the activities will be done from the ground, the halter needs to fit correctly, with the noseband positioned several fingers' width below the bottom of the cheekbones. The noseband should be loose enough for you to slip your hand under it, but no looser. The halter's crownpiece should lie neatly just behind the horse's ears.

A halter controls the horse's head by putting pressure on certain areas. For example, if you were to lead your horse and make a turn to the left, ideally the horse would follow you without any pressure on the halter or lead (we'll get to that part later). However, if you have to encourage your horse with a little tug on the lead rope, she will feel pressure at the top of the crownpiece and along the right side of her face, as you are tugging to left. An improperly fitting halter puts pressure in awkward places, causing your equine partner to be less responsive.

LEAD ROPE

Again, it does not matter whether your lead rope is leather, cotton, or nylon, although I do have a preference for cotton leads, as they have more uses when doing My Horse, My Partner activities. Be sure that whatever lead you use is in good condition and that it is long (or short) enough for you to handle your horse with ease. Standard lead lengths usually suffice. Also preferred for most of the activities are leads without the chains attached, but if leads with chains are all you have, then those can work too.

If you have an aggressive or pushy equine partner, a lead with a chain may actually be preferred for a few activities, so both types may be useful to have on hand. An option, if a chain is needed, is to go to your local hardware or home improvement store and get an eighteen-inch length of medium-weight chain with snaps on each end. Snap the chain on the end of the lead for those few times it might be needed.

SURCINGLE

There are many kinds of surcingles, but the best for our purposes are longeing surcingles with lots of metal rings of various sizes on top and along the sides. A surcingle fits around the girth area of the horse and is used for advanced longeing, beginning driving, and many other training purposes. This is the one piece of equipment many of you may not have, and that's okay. In a pinch, an older English or Western saddle will do. I say older because the saddle will get a lot of use and you don't want to put your best show saddle on and risk it becoming scratched or damaged. The only requirement is that the saddle must fit the horse. We'll talk more about saddle fitting later. Another option is to fasten two or three old cinches or girths together.

SADDLE PADS

For our purposes, a thicker English poly pad or a standard Western pad is best. In a pinch you could use several large, old towels, or cut down a lightweight bed quilt that you find at a thrift store. Again, keep any show pads packed away and make use of older ones, as the pads most likely will become well used.

SADDLES

English, Western, endurance, dressage, cutback, racing, or roping—any style of saddle will work. The fit (discussed later) is key and the saddle, while well broken in, should be in good working order with no loose horns, cracked trees, torn skirts, or other damage.

BRIDLE

Any kind of bridle will work. A bosal or mechanical-style hackamore does not really suit our purposes, but the sidepull type of hackamore is fine. If you are using a bit, a D-ring or eggbutt snaffle works best. Many people like to use O-ring or loose-ring snaffles. I have found O-rings can pinch the corners of some horse's mouths, although an O-ring with rubber bit guards works well. Remember that you will be doing ground training exercises, so even if you are used to riding your horse in a full bridle, or a Pelham, Kimberwicke, curb, or other bit with a shank or curb chain, these ground exercises work best with the abovementioned types of snaffle bits. If you do not have one, a basic snaffle bit can be found at just about any online or retail tack store for under twenty dollars—often you can find one for even less.

LONGE LINES AND DRIVING REINS

Regular longe lines and driving reins of the nylon or cotton variety are fine. If you do not have driving reins, two longe lines will work. The longe lines are a little longer than driving reins, so take extra care that you have them properly gathered. The last thing you want is to trip over the loose end of a longe line. As with the lead ropes, rarely will a longe line with a chain on the end be needed, but you can always use the chain you made for your lead rope, if necessary.

Bit clips allow you to easily clip and unclip toolkit items to a surcingle or saddle. If you do not have any on hand, you can probably rig up something similar.

WHIPS

I consider a whip to be an extension of my arm, not a tool for punishment. In some of the activities, you will tie objects to the end of a whip to help desensitize your partner, or use a whip to guide her through a pattern, so you will find that various lengths of whips, including dressage, driving, and longe, are very helpful. I prefer whips that are white or light gray as these colors usually contrast better with round-pen and arena footings than do the darker varieties, and they are easier for your equine partner to see. However, if black is all you have, that will work, too. Or, if the whip is not something used regularly for show or competition purposes, you could wrap a black dressage or driving whip in white or colored duct tape. I prefer actual whips to some of the commercially marketed "training sticks," because whips have more flexibility and work better for My Horse, My Partner activities.

BIT CLIPS AND LADDER REINS

There are two other pieces of equipment you will need later on. The first are bit clips or similar straps that you can use to clip an object to a saddle or surcingle. They should have clips or snaps at both ends so you can unsnap an item in a hurry, if needed. The straps should be six to ten inches long. In traditional use, the ends of a bit clip are attached to the rings of a bit, and a lead rope is attached to the bit clip's center ring, allowing the handler to lead with pressure on the bit. You can find bit clips in most equestrian catalogs.

The other is a set of ladder reins. Ladder reins look like regular English reins with cross pieces, like rungs on a ladder, every few inches. You can make your own by knotting a few pieces of clothesline across a set of English reins.

FOOTWEAR

It is important for you to wear suitable shoes or boots whenever you are around your horse. This will be pretty obvious to most, but you would be surprised at the number of people who show up at my clinics or who show me a horse while wearing inappropriate footgear. Somehow, they do not understand that it is dangerous to work around horses in shoes or boots with high heels, or in any kind of open-toed shoe. Most horses go out of their way to stay off your feet, but accidents

The ends of ladder reins can be clipped to a saddle or surcingle, then run under your equine partner's tail. It is comparable to a crupper and allows you to eventually hang lightweight items further along your equine friend's back.

These are just a few of the many items you can include in your toolkit.

do happen. Sturdy shoes can make the difference between an unpleasant moment or months in a cast due to a broken bone in your foot.

BEYOND THE BASICS

The following toolkit items are divided into three categories: audio, visual, and movement. Once gathered together, I like to sort them by category into clear plastic storage boxes so I can easily see what I want, but any storage system will work as long as you can quickly find the needed item.

You will also find that some items fit into more than one category. Pom-poms are some of my favorites. If lying on the ground, a pompom will fit into the visual category, but if you are moving it around, a pom-pom makes a rustling sound, so it then can also be considered an audio or a moving item, depending on how it is used. To avoid confusion, sort the item into the category in which you think you will most use it. You can always move it later.

AUDIO

Audio items include anything that makes noise. As you progress through My Horse, My Partner activities, you will learn to tell when your horse likes (or dislikes) listening to certain types of sounds. I once had an Appaloosa mare who showed a definite preference for polka music. Fortunately at the time, I lived in Minnesota, where there are radio stations that actually play polka songs. As you move through the sound-related activities, you may also find specific sounds that scare or anger your equine partner, or that make him nervous. File these sounds away for future reference.

Some of the audio tools I use regularly include a radio and CDs, including the professionally produced "spookless" and "desensitizing" CDs made specifically for horses. Various sizes and shapes of bells, chimes, and rattles also work well. Every size and shape of bell sounds a little bit different, so the more you can find of these, the better. Other suitable noisemakers include children's toys that make noise. The popular See 'n' Say type of toy is great. When you pull a lever, an arrow in the center of the flat, circular toy spins around and eventually points to one of several animals. If it points to a duck, for example, a voice says, "This is a duck. Quack, quack." Other children's toys, such as old handheld video games, or toys that spell words or sing songs, are wonderful to have in your audio toolkit. A toy fishing pole can make a cranking sound when you wind it up, a doll might cry, a teddy bear or action figure might speak, and a fire engine might have a loud siren.

Other household items, such as a small plastic ball in an old pot or metal bucket, make great noises, as do a few rocks inside a plastic milk or water jug, or pieces of tin foil inside a plastic shopping bag. Be creative and think outside the box. A three-ring notebook clapped open and shut makes an interesting sound, as does a musical instrument such as a guitar or a clarinet.

With any of the tools used, it is very important that you check for safety. A child's plastic toy might make a great sound, but if it has a jagged edge from a broken corner, find a similar toy in better shape. You certainly do not want yourself or your horse to be scratched or gouged by a broken edge. Also, check metal items to be sure each is free of sharp edges and rust, and check wooden tools for splinters or protruding nails.

VISUAL

Have you ever led a horse into the same barn day after day with no trouble, only to have her suddenly act like the "boogey man" lives there? Then you know that to a horse, anything can be a visual stimulus. A normal barn item seen out of place or out of context can scare a horse, as can an object she has never seen before.

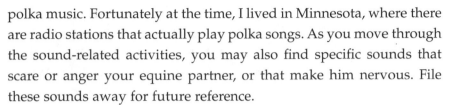

Audio Tools

- Radio
- Spookless CDs
- See 'n' Say
- Squeaky dog toys
- Rattles
- Bells
- Windchimes
- Children's toys
- Pots and pans
- Rocks or balls in a plastic jug or bucket
- Musical instruments
- Rain stick

Visual Tools

- Rain slicker
- Blankets
- Toys
- Frisbee
- Outdoor furniture
- Umbrella
- Balls
- Plastic and paper bags
- Feed sacks
- Buckets
- Hats
- A uniform
- A mailbox
- A flowerpot
- A garden hose

For My Horse, My Partner, we will focus on the odd things your equine partner might occasionally see, such as a plastic bag or a feed sack, an umbrella, an oddly colored slicker, a child's toy, a Frisbee, or a lawn chair. If possible, have several colors or styles of each. White, black, clear, and multicolored plastic can each cause a different reaction, as can a red umbrella versus a yellow one. The key is learning to recognize how your individual horse processes information, which we will discuss as each activity is introduced.

Balls are included in this visual list, and to a horse, a beach ball can look wildly different than a soccer ball, as can a basketball, foam rubber ball, baseball, or polo ball. Buckets and pails are both things you probably have on hand, or can easily find. Grocery bags, funny hats, a uniform, mailbox, pot of flowers, large stuffed animal, and a garden hose can all come in handy. An orange trash bag full of leaves might elicit no reaction from your horse, while a black trash bag full of newspapers is the scariest thing he has ever seen, so the larger variety of objects you can find to put in your visual toolkit and have on hand, the better.

MOVEMENT

Just as many of the audio objects can also fall into the visual category, so can items in both of those categories also be things that move. A beach ball rolling toward a horse is much more frightening than one sitting in a corner of the horse's stall. Plastic makes a noise when blowing in the wind. A slicker rustles oddly when the person wearing it dances. To a horse, a streamer draped across a stall door becomes a completely different object when tied to the end of a dressage whip, as is a wheelchair with someone sitting in it and rolling down the barn aisle, versus the chair sitting in a corner of the grooming area.

Other objects that are great to use when desensitizing for movement include a white plastic or colored foam rubber ball tied to the end of a fishing pole or a longe line. A ball rolling toward or in front of a horse, or even tossed over a horse's back, is an excellent tool. A Frisbee, slinky, or polo mallet work well, as do small bubbles blown toward a horse, or a plastic bag tied to the end of a long rope. And, of course, the old standby, pom-poms, serve a variety of needs.

Many children's toys also have moving parts, including transformers, robots, radio or remote-controlled toy cars, scooters and tricycles, and a child's wagon or baby stroller.

Do you have to have all of the above for you and your horse to benefit from My Horse, My Partner? No, of course not. The items listed are only suggestions. You may find you have just a few of the listed items. On the other hand, you might discover an entirely different set of objects that work well for you.

And speaking of discovering, just where can you get all of these strange items—pom-poms, bells, and rattles? Thrift stores are my first choice. Everything is reasonably priced and you don't have to worry if something breaks, as you do not have a big financial investment in any one item. Yard sales are another great source, as are basements and attics of friends and relatives. Sales at major discount stores are also a possibility, as are area toy stores.

I am a big believer in networking. If you absolutely can't find something you need, ask everyone you know. Sooner or later, someone who knows someone who knows someone will have exactly the right item for you.

Whenever I discover a new tool, I try to anticipate the many different ways it can be used. I also try to think of any way the object could possibly be dangerous to my horse or to me. Know that none of the objects will ever intentionally be used to hurt or scare your equine friend. Instead, she will learn that unique objects and events are not so frightening after all.

Moving Tools

- **Streamers**
- **Balls, rolled or tossed**
- **Objects tied to a rope or pole**
- **Frisbee**
- **Polo or croquet mallet**
- **Bubbles**
- **Plastic bags**
- **Pom-poms**
- **Wheelchair**
- **Children's toys**

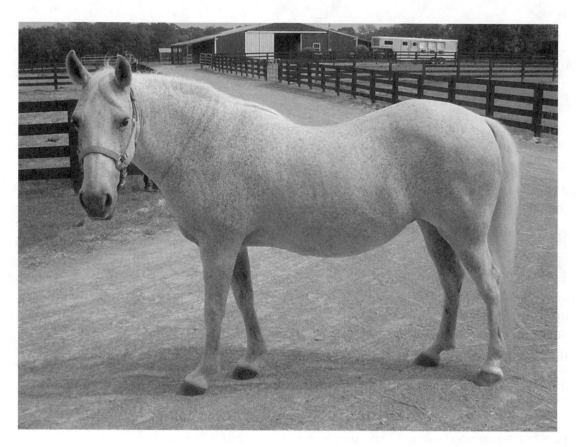

Lady

IT'S A HANDS-ON PROCESS

CHAPTER 2

Allow me to introduce the My Horse, My Partner equine team: Lady, Lucky, Nacho, Nelson, Nomo, and of course, Valentino. This team of horses was chosen from the Saddle Up! herd of more than twenty for their variety in size, age, training, background, and personality. Each has something unique to offer and is probably very much like a horse that you know.

You will be seeing many photos of these horses throughout *My Horse, My Partner* and will get to know them well in the following pages.

LADY

Lady is a 13.2-hand, flea-bitten gray, twenty-two-year-old pony of indeterminate breeding. She came up through the Pony Club and short stirrup circuit and has taught countless numbers of children to ride. Lady is very smart, in the way that many ponies are, and with her advanced years, has become ever so slightly lazy. If I were in her shoes, I can't say I'd choose any differently. She is well trained at the walk, trot, and canter, and is the kind of horse that is confident enough to make her riders ask her correctly.

LUCKY

At the time of the photo shoot for this book, Lucky had been at Saddle Up! for less than a week, and his reactions are very typical of horses

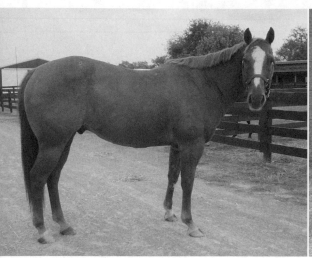

Lucky   Nacho   Nelson

just being exposed to My Horse, My Partner desensitization and training methods. He is a 15.2-hand, thirteen-year-old, copper-colored registered Quarter Horse gelding who used to wow everyone at 4-H shows and in hunter classes. Lucky is very curious and often turns to his human partner for help, but is very sensible even though he is often unsure of new ideas.

NACHO

Nacho is a 14.2-hand, five-year-old chestnut Haflinger gelding with a flaxen mane and tail. Before he came to Saddle Up! he was a driving horse in a Mennonite or Amish community. Nacho has almost too much personality for his own good. He loves to nose through trash cans and play with anything his lips can find. In the two years he has been at Saddle Up! he has enjoyed shredding boxes of tissues, pulling toys out of the arena mailbox, and holding his lead rope in his mouth as he leads himself down the aisle. Haflingers are small draft horses and Nacho, as such, is both gentle and strong-willed. He is also, by nature, very levelheaded. And if Nacho looks somewhat familiar, it is because he was featured in a national print ad campaign for Tractor Supply Company in 2005.

NELSON

If laid-back is your style, then Nelson is your horse. Like Lucky, Nelson is a thirteen-year-old Quarter Horse gelding, but at 16 hands, Nelson is a little taller and he has a bright chestnut coat, rather than copper. Before coming to Saddle Up!, Nelson was a Western pleasure show horse, and then a hunt seat school horse for able-bodied riders.

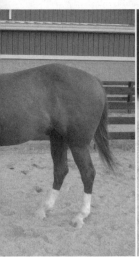
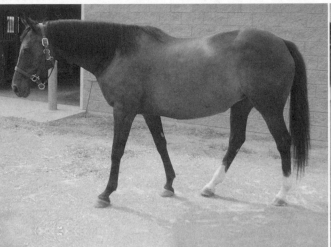
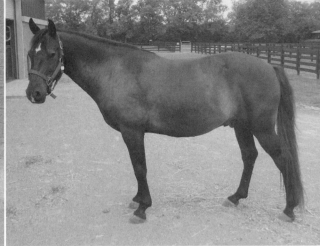

Nomo

Valentino

He is very agreeable and his biggest challenge is staying awake. He has even been known to snooze in the cross-ties.

NOMO

Nomo is a twenty-year-old Thoroughbred mare who has done everything from playing polo to competing in dressage and being a broodmare. Like many Thoroughbreds, she is a little higher strung than the stock-type breeds, but she also tries hard to please and is very nurturing to her human partners. She is a 15.2-hand dark bay.

VALENTINO

You read a lot about Valentino in the previous chapter, but I will add this: he is a people horse. I think if he had his choice, he'd like to be a cat and crawl into your lap. He is smart, gentle, and giving. This horse implicitly trusts people he knows, and while still slow to fully trust new people, his confidence in himself is growing every day.

I know each of the above horses very well, and one method I use to get to know a horse is to get to know his body. You probably have a good working knowledge of your horse's weight, height, and muscle tone, especially if you have spent a few years together, but now it is time to take your knowledge to another level.

THE HANDS-ON PROCESS

Many people imprint foals as soon as they are born. Imprinting is the process of rubbing human hands all over the foal to accustom him to human scent, sound, and touch. The first My Horse, My Partner activity is imprinting of a sort, with an added twist. Because your horse is older than a newborn, he or she has had time to develop likes and dislikes, tastes and preferences, and has been influenced by both good and bad experiences. So in addition to accustoming your equine partner to your scent, sound, and touch, you will take the first step in learning some of her likes and dislikes, and get a baseline reading of her body condition.

It is best to start in a quiet place where your partner is comfortable. It can be a stall, paddock, pasture, grooming area, or wherever your equine friend is at ease. If possible, put on some soft music. And keep your equine partner in mind when choosing both tunes and volume. Just because you like punk or heavy-metal music blasting away, that doesn't mean your partner will. Also, know that your partner's hearing is much better than yours. A volume that sounds normal to you is most likely too loud for your horse. Generally, some soft jazz, classical, or even "elevator music" is a good choice to start with. Remember that you want to use the music to help your partner relax, not gear her up for a polo match.

You can keep your horse's halter on, or not, whatever you are most comfortable with. If you are in a large space, such as a pasture, it will be easier to keep your friend from wandering off if you have a halter and lead. If you are in a stall and feel comfortable and safe without your partner being haltered, then leave it outside the door. If you are uncertain, inexperienced with horses, or feel safety is an issue, you will have the most control over a haltered horse in a medium-sized enclosure such as round pen, or in a grooming area with cross-ties.

Begin by letting your partner sniff the back of your hand. Some horses use their sense of smell a great deal, while others prefer to explore their world by sight, sound, or taste. So this is a good opportunity to gauge your equine friend's use of smell. Of course, before you begin, be sure your hands do not smell like apples, grain, carrots, or any other equine treat. Also be sure your hands do not carry a medicinal smell, or smell like fly spray or any other element your horse may associate with unpleasantness.

Once your partner has satisfied her curiosity by smelling your hand, gently blow into her nostril, and let her blow gently back into yours. This tells your friend that you are interested in relating to her on her level. If you think about it, from day one we expect our equine partners to relate to us on our terms. Rarely do we consider that a horse is a horse, and thinks, acts, and reacts as such. Your horse has spent her entire life watching and studying you. She knows the instant you step into the barn whether you are in a good or bad mood, if you are sad, or whether you are nervous or joyfully happy. But how many of us can say we have the same recognition of our equine friend's thoughts and moods?

Breathing into each other's nostrils is the way that horses instinctively greet each other. When you offer this greeting to her, it is the equine equivalent of spending years in a foreign country and never understanding the language, when a neighbor suddenly speaks to you in English. Immediately, you feel more comfortable knowing someone is attempting to communicate with you in a manner that you understand.

After trading breaths once or twice, it is time to get to know your partner's body. You can begin anywhere, but I like to work front to back and left to right. Begin at the forehead, gently but firmly rubbing and massaging the area with your hands as you talk softly to your friend. What you say is not important, but your tone of voice is. Imagine yourself reassuring a young child, and use that same soft but confident voice. My equine partners usually hear all about the mundane details of my day, or I sometimes tell them stories of other horses, pets, or people in my life. Occasionally, we discuss current events or the weather. And sometimes we just enjoy the silence of each other's company.

After you've spent a minute or two on the forehead, move to your partner's cheeks and then to her ears. From the ears, work your way down the left side of your partner's neck and chest, and run your hands up and down her legs. Then move to the withers, barrel, stomach, and back, always talking softly. You will finish the left side by

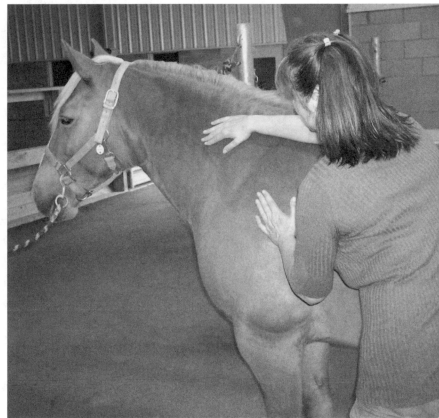

Firm pressure with your hands comforts your partner, and gives you an opportunity to thoroughly learn his or her body.

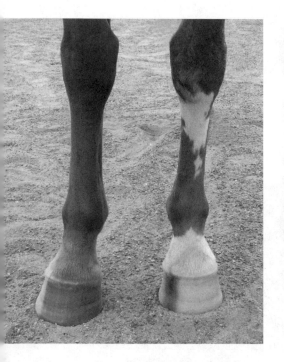

A well-trimmed hoof with no cracks, and no scaly or shelly spots, is an indication of good horse health and nutrition.

Recently, modern science has taken major strides in equine nutrition, and feeds are now formulated for many stages of equine activity and age. Before you begin any training or conditioning program, be sure your equine partner is receiving all the nutrients he needs.

rubbing and gently massaging your partner's loins, croup, flanks, and down the inside and outside of the hind legs. Be sure to remember her tail!

You might also consider switching the music around occasionally to see if one style over another causes her to become more relaxed, excited, or impatient. Music truly is the universal language and you will, over time, be able to find music to both soothe and energize your horse.

While you are rubbing and massaging, also look at your partner's skin tone and make sure the skin is supple—not flaky or scaly. Assess the quality of the hair coat to ensure it is shiny and make note of any bald patches, scars, bumps, indentations, or other blemishes. Look at her hooves to be sure they are in good shape and not cracked or shelly.

If you find anything unusual during your physical assessment, contact your equine veterinarian or your local equine nutritionist. Proper nutrition and veterinary care can make a world of difference in your partner's attitude and performance. Just like you, if your horse does not feel well, or if she is not getting all the vitamins and nutrients she needs, she will not be able to do her best job.

While you are getting to know your equine friend's body, be sure to keep an eye on her ears, her tail, and also the level of her head and neck. Throughout the process, make note of the areas you touch that she likes, and those that make her nervous. You will know she is enjoying it when she leans your way, when her eyes are half closed, or when she emits a soft grunt or groan. If she is relaxed and enjoying the process, her head and neck will be low, her ears will be flicking back and forth as you work, and her tail will be relaxed, possibly swishing slowly at the occasional fly. If something is bothering her, either about your touch or another external factor, her head will be raised, ears possibly flat back, and her tail will swish sharply back and forth. Her body will also be tense and the look in her eye will be anything but soft.

Whenever you get this reaction, stop immediately to assess the problem. What is it about the process that she does not like? Is there a horse behind her that is upsetting her? Maybe the music is making her nervous, or there is a lot of noise and activity in another area of the barn. Does she have a cut or a bruise near the area that you were touching? Bug bites? Does she not like you touching the scar on her right hock? Maybe it is painful to her or invokes memories of a traumatic event. Try moving to a different location or taking your horse on a short walk and resuming again in a few minutes.

When you've finished the left side, repeat the process on the right. At some point, you might find your partner's "sweet spot," that one area where she loves to be brushed. You'll definitely know when you've found it because your partner will lean into your

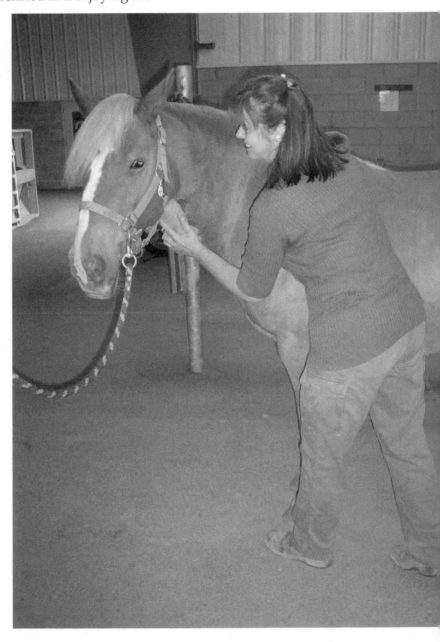

When you find your partner's "sweet spot," brush it often. For Nacho, a turn of the head and sideways ears mean he is intently focused.

touch. She may stretch her neck or even curl her upper lip in pleasure. Nacho, for example, loves to be rubbed vigorously on the front of his neck. Lucky's spot is underneath his mane at the top of his neck. Remember your partner's spot because in the future, scratching the sweet spot can be a wonderful reward for a job well done.

The entire hands-on process will take you fifteen minutes, or maybe even twice that, depending on the size of your equine partner, your size, and how relaxed you both are this first time around. And it is very important that you be relaxed. Horses are herd animals and right now, for this process, you are your horse's herd. As you are the dominant member of the herd, she will look to you for confirmation that this process is safe. So if you are not comfortable doing this, start with a shortened version, and just work on touching her neck and back, or any other area you feel comfortable with. Then gradually work into other areas.

Remember that you and your horse are a team working together to learn about each other and grow in your skills, trust, and confidence. If you sense your equine partner is not accepting one of the My Horse, My Partner activities, you must give her all the time she needs by repeating the process over and over. You must make what is unique routine. And what is unique to one horse—or you—may already be routine to another horse or human partner. Everyone is different. Everyone has had assorted life experiences and has various likes and dislikes. So there will be times that your partner is ready to move on and you are not. That's fine. Just go over and over the process until you are completely comfortable with it. Comfort for you may be achieved in a few days or it may take a month. It is the same for your partner; make sure every activity is fully mastered before going on to the next.

HELPFUL TIPS

Your body posture is a very important part of this process. If you are tense, use rapid strokes, and have an abrupt manner, your horse will sense that something is not quite right and will react by becoming edgy or nervous. Ideally, you should stand and move casually, as if each new activity is no more unusual than sitting down to read the paper. I can't stress enough that your equine partner will take her cues from you. If she senses you are nervous or uncomfortable, she will think there is

Discipline

If you have been around horses for any length of time, you know that a horse may occasionally behave inappropriately—biting, kicking, and crowding are three such behaviors that come to mind, and none of them should be tolerated. However, it is essential to realize that discipline is a three-step process. The first step is to immediately correct the behavior, the second is to evaluate the situation and determine the cause, and the third is to condition your horse toward another response.

If your horse bites, you need to instantly to let her know this is not acceptable. If more than three seconds pass, you will have missed your opportunity for correction. I have found that a combination of voice and action makes it quite clear to any equine partner that her behavior is intolerable. A sharp "no" along with stern and prolonged eye contact is often sufficient. A sharp jerk on the halter can reinforce the message, but continual jerking of the halter or manhandling of the horse does not accomplish anything. The next step is to determine the cause of the action.

If your partner snapped or bit at you when you were touching a specific part of her body, she's probably sore. She may have been giving you warning signals, such as pinned ears or a swishing tail, that you ignored, or if you suddenly made contact with the sore spot her reaction could have been just as quick. This is her way of telling you it hurts.

On the other hand, if you are dealing with a horse that is lazy and spoiled, you can encourage your partner toward a less violent reaction by combining instant correction with positive reinforcement for the good actions she takes. This is can be a lengthy process, during which you provide only black or white responses. This means no gray areas in your partner's mind about her behavior: if the action was good, she is praised. Not good, she is immediately corrected.

A few horses have been badly abused and are, frankly, dangerous. If you are an experienced horseperson, trust your instincts and find the horse another home if you know you can't handle the horse safely. If you are inexperienced, get the opinion of a professional or two. Sometimes the difference between spoiled and dangerous is hard to determine. Spoiled can usually be helped. Dangerous usually cannot. A dangerous horse is one whose regular unpredictability causes harm, or the potential for harm, to her human partner. The horse does not have to be mean or aggressive to be dangerous. A sweet horse who is terrified of cars and trucks can be a danger, as can a horse who regularly kicks, bucks, rears, or bolts.

Equine discipline can be quite a complex undertaking, and there are many good books and videos that cover the subject matter in detail. My Horse, My Partner helps you and your equine friend build trust and confidence in each other, so many behavior problems will diminish as you progress through the activities.

something to be nervous and uncomfortable about. So talk softly, stay relaxed and pretend any new idea you introduce is very routine.

The same is true for a pleasant facial expression. Whether you know it or not, your equine partner is a great interpreter of your face. She understands your smile, cold look, indifference, anger, joy, and pain, far more than you realize. Remember, horses study us far more than we study them. It is critical to her survival that she know whether you are about to lash out in frustration, or if you are simply using her shoulder to cry on. A soft and pleasant expression on your face will help your equine friend relax and be confident that any new concept you introduce will not be anything to be concerned about.

Another key concept is working in rhythm. If you have ever had a massage, you know how relaxing and monotonous the kneading of the massage therapist's hands can be if she gets a good rhythm going. The same notion applies here. In addition to the soothing concept of rhythm, your partner anticipates rhythm. Imagine yourself sweeping the barn aisle. After a few strokes you make a virtually identical repetitive action every time you sweep. Once you find your rhythm, a horse will anticipate the measured sound of the broom hitting the ground and pushing the stray pieces of dust and bedding over and over again. After a time, when nothing terrible happens, the sound and rhythm become soothing to your friend.

This concept is important to keep in mind every time you introduce something new to your equine partner. Whether it is rubbing your hands over her body, or desensitizing her to a plastic bag, do it in rhythm with a relaxed body posture and a pleasant facial expression, and your horse will accept it much more quickly and with much less stress.

SAFETY

It is important to remember that even the most trusted horse in the world might cause you to be injured. When I was thirteen or so, I was picking out my horse's left front foot when she lifted her left rear to smack a fly that had landed on her belly. But instead of the fly, she got me right in the middle of my forehead and knocked me out cold. Obviously, this was a freak accident. This was a horse who would never intentionally hurt me, and how often does a horse balance on its two

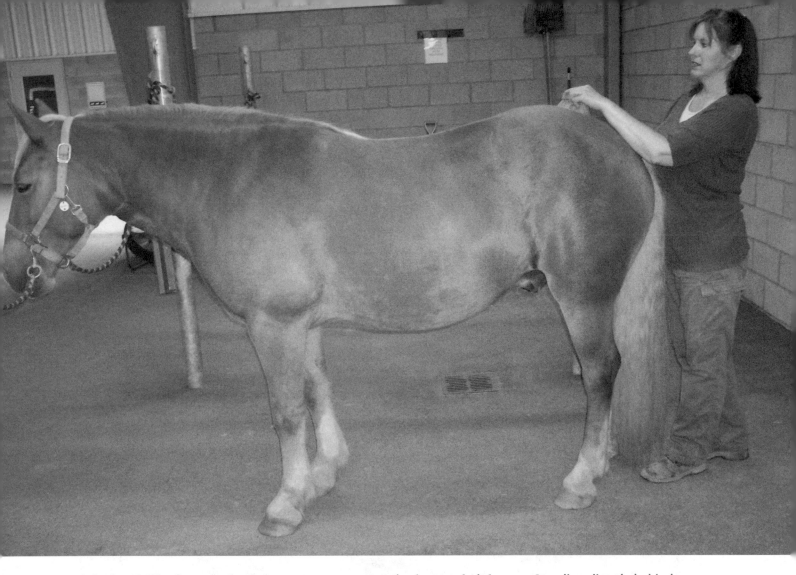

right legs? The fly must have been very annoying for her to shift her balance like that, and my head just happened to be in the way. While an inherent risk is always present when working with horses, there are a few basic things you can do to maximize the safety factor for both you and your partner.

I've already mentioned proper footwear. Low heels, a solid toe, enough said. It is also a good idea to stay away from the front and rear of a horse for the simple reason that those areas are blind spots. If you draw a line from the sides of your partner's eyes out to a point about four feet in front of her, that is an area that she can't see. If you sometimes see your horse turning her head to look at an object in front of her, that's why. She can't see an object if she is looking at it straight on, unless it is far enough away to overcome the blind spot.

The same goes for the rear of the horse. Horses can see quite a ways alongside their hindquarters, but not directly behind them. How much a horse sees also depends on his or her build. A heavily muscled Quarter Horse will not see as much behind him as a more slightly built Arabian or Saddlebred.

Standing directly behind a horse is unsafe because horses cannot see directly behind them. Even though Nacho looks sleepy here, if he became startled I could get hurt.

Obviously, staying away from the front and back areas of a horse is wise. If you have to move into those areas, be sure to move quietly and calmly, touch and talk to your partner as you move, and stay in fairly close. Kicking is like swinging a baseball bat. To hit the ball hard, you have to make a big swing. To kick hard, the horse needs a big area to swing her leg.

I also encourage you to stay away from your partner's nose and mouth. I know it is fun to hand-feed your equine partner treats, but it distracts her from other activities. Many horses move their lips, trying to bite whatever you have in your hand, anytime you move your hand toward their mouth, even to brush their noses or trim the hair of their chin. If this is the case, she is not thinking about standing quietly, or listening to what you are saying to her. Instead, she is thinking only of what goodie you might have for her. One thing she definitely is not concentrating on is her training. So if you feed treats, I suggest doing so from a bucket.

A safe work space is important. This outdoor ring, while large, offers good sandy footing and the post and rail fencing is well maintained.

Some people unconsciously play with their horse's nose and mouth by wiggling their fingers on the soft part of the horse's nose. The horse then moves its nose and lips and it is very cute to watch. But look at it from the horse's perspective. What if every time your human partner came up to you she wiggled her fingers on your nose? Wouldn't you get tired of it after a while? If a horse tires of the action, her only options are to jerk her head away, strike out, kick, or bite. The action also encourages the horse to become tense when you arrive because she expects you to do something that makes her uncomfortable. Because I prefer my equine partner to think positively of me, and not the treats I offer, I stay away from the nose and mouth whenever possible.

Your working environment is also a concern. The old adage that you can turn a horse loose in an empty, padded stall and she will find a way to hurt herself has a grain of truth. With that in mind, it is important to thoroughly check your working area for loose nails, splinters, rusty metal, rocks, holes, and other sources of danger.

While not everyone has access to perfect facilities, you can make what you have the best it can be. I trained at one barn in Washington state that had rocky turnout paddocks attached to each stall, and I was constantly picking rocks from those paddocks. While it was time-intensive, I know the rock picking saved my horses from possible stone bruises

While older, this round pen is the perfect size for many My Horse, My Partner activities. Its panels and joints are solid and the footing is free of rocks and holes.

and abscesses. Would I have preferred a sandy loam footing for the paddocks? Sure, but you work with what you have.

RESULTS!

If you have completed this first My Horse, My Partner activity you will have learned many things about your horse, and your horse will have learned many things about you. First, you will have established a baseline on her weight, muscle tone, and condition, as well as the condition of her skin and hooves. If your partner loses muscle over her back, develops a rash, or has changes in a scar, you will know.

You will also have found where your equine friend likes and doesn't like to be touched, where she is ticklish, and what tone of voice and type of touch she prefers. You will also have noted her musical likes and dislikes, which will be a big help when you begin desensitizing for sound, and which can help keep her calm during times of illness or stress.

Your partner, on the other hand, will understand that you are trying to communicate in a way she understands, and she will appreciate that effort. While we humans are the dominant partner, in many ways we are the less perceptive. Horses observe so much—about us, and the environment in which we live—that we humans completely overlook. From weather to dangerous situations to the mood shifts of humans and animals, horses are much smarter than we.

Hopefully, you and your equine partner will review this first activity often, as it can be an enjoyable quiet time for you both. In the meantime, you are now ready for the next activity.

MORE THAN JUST A SACK

Horses see objects differently than humans do. We often forget this fact, but we shouldn't. Because humans cannot actually see the world through the eyes of a horse, we can't conclusively say horses see a certain way, but we can make some educated guesses.

One of those guesses has to do with color. Because horses have just two cones in their eyes that process color, while humans have three, it is thought that horses do not see colors the same way humans do. However, horses probably do see some color. What colors those are remain debatable, but I am in agreement with Dr. Temple Grandin, author of *Animals in Translation*, that horses best see colors in the yellow/green range and in the blue/purple range. My thoughts do not have any scientific base, but in working with the many items in My Horse, My Partner activities, I've observed that horses seem to better see objects in those color ranges.

A known difference between the way horses and humans see is that humans use binocular vision. That means because our eyes are at the front of our head, we see things with both eyes, and our brain then processes the images from our two eyes into one picture. Because horses' eyes are set on the sides of their heads, horses have both binocular and monocular vision. This means your equine friend can see separate images with his left and right eye, and his brain will process each individually. And, if he is looking straight ahead, a horse can see binocularly, with both eyes, and his brain will process the separate pictures from each eye into one image.

When a horse uses monocular vision he loses depth perception, or the ability to judge how far away an object is. So if a horse sees a potentially scary object from his right eye, even if it is thirty feet away, he may perceive that object as being two feet away. Many people also believe that horses do not see clearly out of all areas of their eyes. The clearest vision seems to be through a horizontal band across the middle of the eye, with blurry areas above and below. That's why you sometimes see your equine partner raising and lowering his head as he stares at a car or a dog in the distance. He is focusing on the moving object in the clearest areas of his eye. That's also why some horses spook when they see a moving object in their blurry range; they cannot tell what it is until their head is positioned to see the object more clearly. The spooking, in this case, is an instinctive and protective reaction.

Because horses probably see a more limited color range than humans do, they see the world in sharper contrasts. For example, if you walk your equine partner across a cement driveway, the darker grooves that join the pieces of pavement together may, to your partner, seem like a bottomless crevasse. No wonder he is reluctant to cross! And, because a horse's eye is very large, it is slow to adjust to light differences. If your horse hesitates before going into a dark stall or a trailer, it's simply because it looks to him like a completely black box. You would hesitate, too, if someone led you up to a doorway and all you could see inside was utter darkness. All of this brings us to the next My Horse, My Partner activity: desensitizing your equine partner to various sights.

More than a hundred years ago, cowboys would gently slap their young horses with a saddle pad before putting the saddle on the first few times. This was to teach the horse that the pad was nothing to be afraid of, and that it would not hurt them.

Horses today regularly see a great deal more of life than the range horses of yesteryear did. Much of what those horses saw were elements found in nature: cows, wildlife, and maybe a few coyotes or wild horses. While they did need to accept ropes thrown over their head, campfires, and other ranch activities, they did not come across the many different man-made elements that today's horse's do. Today's horse sees just about everything we see: cars, balloons, tricycles, umbrellas, plastic bags, and soccer balls. Because your horse will potentially encounter all of these things (and more!), it is important to desensitize him not just to a saddle pad, but also to as many things as possible.

ONE EASY OBJECT

A good item to start with is a neutral or pastel-colored washcloth or small towel. The color is important because you want your equine partner to be able to see it clearly, but not be overwhelmed by the color. Black or white cloth can provide too much of a contrast and bright, intense colors can intimidate some horses at this stage.

Washcloths are also good because they do not make much noise. Plastic crinkles and rustles, and larger towels can actually make a whistling noise or land with a thud on your partner's back as you toss it over his body. Additionally, a horse will perceive a larger object as being scarier than a smaller one.

A round pen is a good place to begin this activity. If you don't have one, a large stall or a paddock will do. Be sure your partner's halter is on and adjusted properly, and that your lead rope is in good working order. Remember your casual body position and pleasant facial expression, and let your equine friend smell the cloth. Once he is satisfied that it is a safe object, begin by rubbing it all over his body, just as you did with your hands in the last activity. Use soft background music if you have found something that relaxes your partner, and talk softly to him as you work.

As with the previous activity, your partner may tell you he is uncomfortable with you touching him in certain areas. He will tell you this by tensing up, raising his head, pinning his ears, or swishing his tail. As long as you are certain no immediate medical attention is needed in these areas, ignore them for now. We will have a special activity for them in Chapter Five.

Your equine friend may try to walk away from you as you go through this process. It is okay to allow a few steps, as you do not want to make him feel confined. If it is more than a few steps, however, gently pull your partner's head back around toward you. You want to be sure his attention is on you and the cloth, and walking away can be an avoidance tactic.

An important safety note here is to be sure your lead rope (if you are using one) is coming up through the bottom, or heel, of your hand, and that its first point of contact is not through your fingers. This gives you added control in case your equine friend gives you a good, solid tug. If your partner should ever manage to pull you off balance or begin running, just let go. Nothing is worth being dragged and, as you are in an enclosed area, you will be able to quickly catch your partner, calm him, and resume the activity. If this behavior is routine for your friend, then a session or two with a lead shank or chain can be helpful. A quick tug and release with a lead chain usually brings your partner's attention back to you. Be sure to avoid a steady pull whenever using a lead chain, as continual pressure will reduce its effectiveness.

After you have rubbed the cloth all over your partner's body, stand to his left side with the lead rope held as a figure eight in your left hand (be sure never to coil the rope around your fingers), and gently and repeatedly slap the cloth onto your partner's midsection.

Your equine friend will most likely react in one of three ways. He might flinch slightly and try to walk away, he may attempt a mad dash for the nearest exit, or he may stand there as if nothing happened. Whatever the reaction, your job is to show your partner that everything is just fine, and you do this with your pleasant facial expression, firm voice, casual body posture, and the repeated and steady gentle tossing of the cloth against your horse's side.

We talked earlier about the importance of rhythm, and it is a central factor here. A steady, consistent rhythm will help your partner relax and anticipate the next swing of your arm. If you have music, swinging your arm to the beat of the music also helps. Horses learn by association, and listening to music he likes will help him associate this process with something he already perceives as pleasant. (i.e., you are teaching him to associate the cloth with pleasant music and safety, rather teaching him to give in to his natural instinct, which is to flee from the scary object.)

Be sure, too, that at this early stage you are using an underhand movement with your arm, rather than an overhand one. An underhand movement is the least threatening arm gesture you can make. After all, how often does a person beat a horse using an underhand arm movement? If your horse has ever been abused or seen another horse being abused, it most likely was by someone using a side or overhand arm movement. To a horse, underhand is generally safe.

Remember that this exercise is not designed to frighten your partner, but to accustom him or her to the possibility of plastic flying toward him on a trail ride, or the rider of another horse removing a windbreaker. This is also an exercise in trust. He will learn to trust that you will not hurt him and you learn to trust that he will react calmly

Positioning the Chain

If you decide to use a chain, know that there is an ongoing debate whether to thread the chain over or under the nose. The answer really depends on the individual horse and the situation, but in this instance I prefer under. Here's why: most horses are trained to move away from pressure, but pushy horses often move into it. If a chain is threaded over the nose, a pushy horse will push up, into the pressure, which may create a bad habit of throwing his head up. When the chain is placed under his nose, if a pushy horse pushes against it all that happens is that he drops his head. Additionally, the skin on top of a horse's nose is more tender than the skin underneath his chin. So, placing a chain on top of a pushy horse's nose has a greater chance of pinching the skin.

Not every horse needs a chain—in fact, the vast majority do not. However, if your partner does not listen well, then a session or two with the chain can be helpful. And remember, your partner only feels the pressure of the chain if he does not respond correctly and with respect to your cues.

To correctly position the chain, thread it through the left opening by the halter's noseband, through the bottom halter ring, through the opening on the right side of the halter, then (if the chain is long enough) up to the opening on the right between the throatlatch and the headstall. When you give a quick tug and release, it puts pressure not only under the chin, but along the poll as well. You can also attach the end of the chain to the opening on the right side of the halter's noseband, which provides less pressure on the poll, but provides stronger control than a regular lead. If you are using a normal lead, attach it as usual to the bottom ring on the halter.

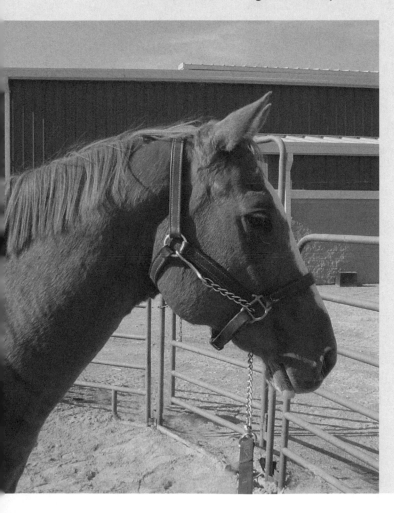

If used properly, a lead rope with a chain on the end can sometimes help your partner. Lucky is wearing his properly, with the end of the chain run up the far side of the halter and under the chin. A second option is to run the chain over the nose.

to the unexpected. You both are at the very beginning of this process, but it is a step toward making many unique events routine.

Your partner may accept this repeated and gentle rhythmic slapping instantly, or it may take a few sessions. You will know your partner has accepted it once he stands quietly on a loose lead with his head relatively low, and does not flinch when the cloth makes contact. Hopefully, he will also lick or smack his lips. This is a very good indication of submission and acceptance in a horse. Lucky, the Quarter Horse who is still new to Saddle Up!, is at the point where he is doing a lot of licking and smacking. He often is not sure what I want him to do, but he is telling me that he is trying to understand and is doing his best to cooperate.

Once your equine partner accepts the "sacking" procedure on his barrel, you can begin to vary the location of contact. Move to the neck and down the legs, but stay away from your equine friend's face, as he will be extra protective of his eyes and ears.

If your partner is of the excitable type, you might continue for several minutes and then take a break to let your friend think about things for a while. I have found that even if I do not believe I am making progress, if I leave a horse alone to think things over, he often has processed the information positively by the time I return a few minutes later. If your partner is a more accepting fellow, you might continue for ten or more minutes. Remember, you are still just on the left side and using a soft underhand motion.

Regardless of the time, you can stop as soon as your equine friend shows acceptance; there really is no point in continuing once he understands the process. Your friend's licking and smacking his lips, soft eye, relaxed body, lowered head, and swiveling ears all indicate that he is willing. Not all signs have to be present, but over time you will come to understand your partner's individual signals of acceptance very well. Your partner may need several sessions before you see signs of full acceptance, but if you see significant progress you can move to the right side of your friend.

I think horses are interesting creatures for a variety of reasons, but one element I find fascinating is that the left and right sides of their brains do not connect as the brains of most other mammals do. So what you teach on the left side of the horse you must also teach on the right side. This is why many horses are fine being led from the left but refuse to move when being led from the right. To a horse, being led from the right is a completely different concept and must be taught separately. More on that later.

So everything you did on the left, you will now do on the right, again making note of the areas your partner readily accepts the cloth, and areas he does not.

TAKE IT UP A NOTCH

Once your equine friend has accepted the light slapping of the cloth in an underhand movement over all parts of his body, it is time to step it up. The second part of this activity is to repeat the process using a soft sidearm movement. Remember that this movement is a little more threatening to a horse, so start with a slow arm, gradually working up to faster speeds. Again, your horse may accept this immediately, or it may take several sessions. You can also now include the back and rump, areas that are hard to reach using an underhand movement.

The final step with the washcloth is to use an overhand arm movement. Keep in mind that your horse may see this as a threatening gesture from you, so the relaxed body posture and pleasant voice and facial expression are all the more important.

When Nacho first came to Saddle Up! we completed this entire activity in about five minutes. He never once flinched during any of it. He was absolutely non-reactive and was more interested in eating the cloth than protecting himself by flinching or moving away. Being a Haflinger and of draft stock makes Nacho more accepting than many other horses. Besides, flinching is a lot of work! We occasionally review this activity together, but it really is more for my benefit than his. I want to be sure he has retained the training, which for him, is really his natural acceptance of things.

Nomo, on the other hand, needs regular review work. Having been a broodmare makes her naturally more protective, and her nature as a Thoroughbred is more energetic than that of Haflinger. In a horse's very matriarchal society the skills Nomo developed as a mother now transfer to "herd-watcher." Instead of watching over and protecting her babies, Nomo now feels it is her job to watch over and protect her herd. Like many mares, Nomo's preservation instincts are stronger than a gelding's, so she benefits from having a quick review session every month or so.

Pom-poms come in many shapes, sizes, and colors and can be used in a variety of ways.

USING YOUR TOOLKIT ITEMS

Once your equine partner has fully accepted the light tossing of the washcloth all over his body, you can move on to other items in your toolkit. Good items for this next step include anything light, flexible, and soft, such as a bag or pom-pom. For now, use only an object that you hold in your hand. For example, tying a plastic bag to a stick is not a good idea at this point, although it won't be too much longer before you and your horse are ready for that.

Plastic bags, feed bags, and grocery bags come in all sorts of shapes, sizes, and colors, which is a great opportunity to further determine colors that your horse prefers, those he might have difficulty seeing, and those that make him leery. The same goes for pom-poms. Every high school, college, and sports team has its own pom-pom in a unique color and style, and each will look different to your partner.

Remember that to a horse, each new object poses a new threat. Our goal is not to frighten your friend, but to accustom him to so many different items that when he encounters something new, he reacts with healthy curiosity rather than instinctive fear.

In using a pom-pom or a bag you will also be introducing a new element: sound. Each bag will sound different, and the varied motions you make will also produce diverse noises. So in addition to watching your partner closely to determine his reactions to shapes and colors, you will be watching for his reactions to, and preferences for, sound.

Start in the same manner you did with the washcloth, by letting him see and smell the object in your hand. Then gently rub your partner's barrel. Finally, increase the area to other parts of your horse's body. Once he accepts the object in the rubbing phase, move to the gentle, rhythmic tossing.

Your equine partner might not be comfortable with this process at all. In that case, let your horse figure it out on his own by putting him in a stall or other small enclosure with the object. For example, if your horse is especially afraid of black plastic, you can line his feed bucket with it, or put it underneath a flake of hay. Food motivates even the most hesitant equine friend. Depending on his level of acceptance, you may have to continue this for several days, or even a week. It is all about making the unique routine. When it becomes routine for your horse to eat on top of black plastic, acceptance will come.

Another idea is to put your partner in a stall and drop eight or ten plastic bags on the floor of the stall. We did this when Valentino first came to Saddle Up!, and at first he was afraid to move a muscle. But eventually he got hungry and thirsty, and those needs were more powerful than his fear of the plastic. Before too long he was stepping on the bags as if they were the shavings the rest of his stall was bedded in.

At first it is good to monitor your equine friend from a distance, to be sure he or she does not panic. Sometimes one bag on the stall floor is enough for an initial attempt. This is also a good time to watch your horse as he thinks through this problem. Does he turn his head to the side for a different viewpoint? Does he bob his head up and down, or raise it very high and look down his nose at the objects? Your partner might take a tentative sniff and then back away, or move sideways. Is he very bold, dropping his nose under the item for further inspection? Does he lick it, taste it, or blow on it?

And how does he indicate acceptance? Does he give a big sigh?

It is important to stand where you can see your partner's ears and body, and to develop a regular, but casual, rhythm.

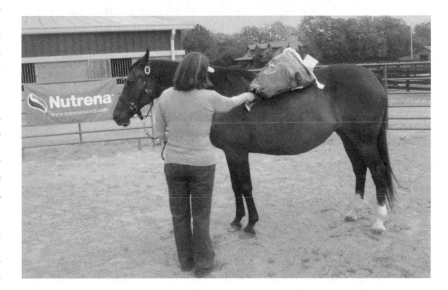

Nomo's ears indicate she is focused on the movement and sound of the feed sack that is gently and rhymically touching her body. Her lowered head tells me she is not overly concerned.

Smack his lips? Give a big swish of his tail or drop his head? These are important clues for you in getting to know your partner on an entirely new level. As you progress further through My Horse, My Partner activities, and as you spend the coming days, weeks, and years with your equine partner, each new challenge you encounter together can be eased if you understand what your horse is telling you. So the more time you can spend observing your equine friend, the better.

Playing

A WORD OF CAUTION: once your horse accepts any new object, he or she will most likely begin to show some curiosity. I once had a two-year-old gelding who, once he realized there was nothing to fear, decided he really liked to shred plastic into little tiny pieces. I wasn't so concerned about the cleanup factor as I was about the possibility of him swallowing some of it.

Playing is good. Your partner obviously is not afraid of an object if he grabs it in his teeth and dashes it against the ground. But as with a small child, play needs to be supervised so he does not get carried away and break something or get hurt.

For example, let's say your horse reacts to the black plastic by initially ignoring it, then blowing on it, pawing it, and finally stepping on it. If you encounter a bridge on a trail ride and your partner turns away, he is telling you he wants to ignore it. If you can get him to the blowing stage, all you have to do is be patient as he goes through his individual stages of acceptance. And because you understand the stages, you won't reprimand him when he reaches out a tentative hoof to paw at the bridge. You understand him enough to know that this is a stage in his acceptance process. Every horse is different. Pawing from another horse might be an indication that he is impatient, frustrated, or nervous. But in this instance with this horse, pawing can be a good sign.

FUN WITH NOISES

When it comes to horses there is no consistent timeline. What Nacho accepted in five minutes might take another horse a month. When your equine partner has accepted all the plastic bags and pom-poms you can find, or the equivalent thereof, it is time to move on.

Next, move into the sound category, and introduce bells, rattles, and toys that make noise. The only difference here is that you will never use the underhand, sidearm, or overhand motion of lightly and rhythmically slapping your partner with these items. Anything other than a soft object has the potential to hurt your partner, so you want to stay with just gentle rubbing.

When introducing a sound object, make sure you hold the item quietly at first. Be sure your partner is haltered so you can keep his head toward you and keep him from walking off. Avoidance is a tactic many horses (and people) like to use. Once your equine partner has accepted the object by sniffing and inspecting it, then you can gently shake it to make noise. Remember your casual body posture and your rhythm. Sometimes, if your partner is a little nervous, it is helpful to lead him around a small enclosure such as a round pen or paddock as you gently shake the object, rather than asking him to remain still.

And again, if your partner is unusually uncomfortable, place the object in his feed bucket for a few days. Just be sure the item is big enough that it can't be eaten, or that it won't break into pieces if dropped. A few days in the feed bucket or within sight of the stall usually turns the scary thing into a curiosity factor, or even something boring. If your partner begins to play with it, it is time to take the object away.

In addition to bells, toys, and rattles, some noisemakers include an alarm clock, a soft buzzer, a ringing telephone, or professionally produced CDs with a variety of pre-recorded sounds such as mooing cattle, gunshots, and clanging gates. For these sound objects, I find it easier to leave the horse in his stall while the human partner and object are outside and nearby. Especially if the sound is one that is continual, such as the CDs, or can be made to repeat frequently, such as the ringing of a phone, it's best to let your equine partner figure out for himself that these are non-threatening noises.

MOVING OBJECTS

Objects that move can run the gamut from flags and balls to radio-controlled cars and umbrellas. And, as with sound, these are not objects you want to toss at your partner. The introduction process should now be routine for you and your horse. When you are both ready you can begin movement slowly. If the object is a streamer or flag, wave it gradually and gently, and not too close to your equine partner's body. If you are working with a ball, roll it slowly across your horse's line of vision. You can gradually work in closer and move the object faster.

Your horse will want to inspect an umbrella in both the closed and open positions, and may want to inspect any moving object over and over again. He should be free to inspect as frequently as he wants. Be sure a ball does not roll so fast that it pops up and bumps him in the nose, or that any of the umbrella parts poke him in the side.

As you progress from one object to the next, you will eventually notice that your equine friend is accepting new things more quickly. This is happening for several reasons. One, he has now had enough experience with this process that he is beginning to trust that you will not bring him anything that poses a danger. And two, he has created enough reference points in his brain to know that this new object truly is not scary.

You may also have realized that your horse is slower to accept items that are a certain color, for example, yellow. You can then help him by feeding from a yellow bucket, wearing a yellow shirt, or providing yellow objects in his stall. He may have been abused by someone wearing yellow or had a yellow bucket blow into him during a windstorm. He then mistakenly associates being hit with the color yellow. By providing your equine partner safe points of "yellow" reference, you are gradually negating the previous traumatic effect that the color had.

RESULTS!

Depending on your partner's nature and personality, this activity is one you might work on for several weeks and rarely revisit, or this may become a regular part of the time you spend together. If you are a horse, there are always new things to see and inspect!

Through this activity you should have learned how your horse initially responds to the unknown, and how he works through problems. You've learned his unique signals of acceptance and his preferences in colors, sound, and movement. You've also learned what types of objects he is likely to reject, ignore, or find just plain boring.

Your equine partner, on the other hand, is learning to trust you. He has been exposed to countless different objects and his understanding and acceptance has made him more confident in his abilities.

In the next activity you will move away from desensitization and work on respect, which is key to further progress.

CHAPTER 4

THE MOST IMPORTANT WORD ON THE PLANET

You may be wondering why you have not been encouraged to work on the more sensitive areas of your horse's body, such as the ears. Those are the body parts that your equine partner is most uncomfortable with you touching, so why not spend more time desensitizing those spots? The answer is respect. Your partner has to respect you a bit more before she will be comfortable with you touching those areas, and gaining that respect is the focus of this next activity.

Understanding that "whoa" means "stop right now, no questions asked," is very important. I personally will not get on a horse that does not respond correctly to the word. I also will not longe or ground drive a horse who does not stop when asked while being led. Over my many decades working with horses, I have seen too many people and horses become hurt simply because a horse has not been taught or does not respect the word whoa.

I teach horses and students to respond both to a voice cue and a hand cue. Several times I have been in places where a loudspeaker or noise from a crowd made it difficult for my horse to hear me, but a hand signal saved the day. A hand signal can also make it easier to catch your equine partner, if she is the type who likes to make a game of it.

Approaching from eleven o'clock, I am ahead of Lucky's center of gravity. The hand signal is an added cue for him to stay put.

Let me give you a few examples of how an unquestioning stop response to whoa might save you or your horse from harm. Many years ago I was giving a saddleseat riding lesson to a seven-year-old girl on a very round, flat-withered Appaloosa mare during the heat of summer. After half an hour or so the mare was slick with a light sweat. Even though I had checked the girth a few times, when the mare came around the corner of the arena at a nice, slow canter, the saddle slipped. My young student was now hanging off the side of a cantering horse. Fighting my urge to panic, I held up my hand as a person controlling traffic would do, called the mare's name and said "whoa." With a clear look of relief, the mare stopped and my student dropped safely to the ground.

More recently, I was watching a riding lesson at Saddle Up! when the instructor of a teenage boy felt he was ready to trot independently, off-lead. The boy had been walking, steering, and stopping independently quite well for some time, and trotting well with a leader controlling the horse, Rosie, a retired Thoroughbred polo pony. When the time came to trot off-lead, the boy purposely kicked Rosie hard in the ribs, leaned forward, and yelled, "Yah!"

Of course, Rosie did just exactly as she was told to do, and broke into a canter. But as she moved into the three-beat gait, the boy became frightened and began shrieking. The loud noise alarmed Rosie and I could see her eyes widen as she threw up her head and extended her stride. Before things could get out of hand, however, the instructor held up his hand and firmly said, "Rosie, whoa." And Rosie stopped.

In the first instance the misplaced saddle could have panicked the mare and she could have bucked the young girl off. Or, the child could have gotten a foot stuck in a stirrup and been dragged. In the second story the frightened horse could have run through fencing, causing serious injury to herself and her rider, if he had stayed on that long. In each case, the horse wanted guidance from her human partner and responded well when it was given.

Lastly, I had a student who was hauling her horse to a trail ride some miles away. Something happened en route and the horse went down in the trailer, wedging himself so tightly that an emergency rescue crew had to be called to cut the trailer apart to get him out. I happened by the scene and stopped to help. Imagine my surprise when I found my student in the trailer with her terrified horse, using her hand signal and calmly saying "whoa" every minute or so. The horse was visibly shaking, but he did not move, even when the metal saw cut mere inches above his head. The horse had numerous lacerations and abrasions, but eventually healed completely. Two months later, my student and her horse went on their trail ride and, fortunately, this time there were no mishaps along the way.

TEACHING WHOA

As you can see, it is imperative that your partner learn the correct response to "whoa," and teaching that response starts on the ground with a halter and lead rope. If your equine friend is the pushy kind, then this is one time you may wish to trot out the lead chain. Begin in a round pen or other fairly small area. Face the same direction your partner is facing and, as you begin to walk, verbally ask your partner to walk with you by saying, "walk," or "walk on." Walk a few steps, then ask your horse to stop, first by stopping, then saying "whoa," and finally (if needed) pulling back on the halter. Ideally, your partner should stop the instant you stop walking. If your equine friend does not stop neatly and cleanly when you stop, say "whoa" and pull back. If she still does not listen, then a session or two with the chain will help greatly. Be sure to let your partner know when she has done something right, by patting her neck, or saying "good girl."

Depending on what part of the country you live in and the type of riding you do, you might use the word "ho" instead of whoa. Either will do, as it is the tone of voice and the long "o" vowel sound your equine friend is responding to, not the actual word. You could just as easily say, "no," "go," "doe," or "so," and your friend will respond in exactly the same manner. When I was in college we had a retired reining horse in the barn. One of my fellow students was loping him around the indoor arena when a friend came in and greeted the rider. The rider responded by calling out, "hello." As you may have guessed, the old horse put on the brakes and the rider somersaulted off the front of the horse. Luckily, he landed on his feet, no worse for the experience.

POSTURE COUNTS

Just as your body posture was important during the desensitization process, your posture, facial expression, and language are just as important here, but in a different way. With this activity you want to be very businesslike. Stop short of being abrupt, but your horse needs to know that it is time to work, rather than time to play. You will best accomplish this by having a neutral expression on your face. Before, you wanted to be pleasant, because you were introducing concepts that were new and potentially scary to your equine partner. Here, you want your friend to see by your face that you are going to be a little firmer.

Your posture should also be more purposeful, and your movements a bit quicker. Remember that your equine partner studies you far more than you study her, so she will know, just by looking at you, that it is time to get focused. At first it can be difficult to maintain a good balance between being gentle but firm, and between kindness and authority. But with some practice, you will find the right mix for your partner, and it will get easier.

Practice the walk/whoa (or ho) combination over and over and over again, until your equine friend understands that nothing else is an option. Her only choice is to stop. Some horses will pick it up in a few minutes; others will take longer.

Remember, too, that your partner wants and seeks guidance from you. With these activities, you are establishing yourself as the dominant one in this partnership, so your equine friend will begin to turn to you more and more for guidance. Even though you may not see it yet, she wants you to tell her what to do, and she wants to do it. If, however, your horse is currently presenting a little challenge, here are a few tips that will help you through the rough spots.

- **Never vary the routine.** Horses learn through consistency. Stop walking, use the verbal directive "whoa," and then give a little tug on the halter. It is as easy as that. Eventually your partner will stop when you do and no cues will be needed. That is your goal. But for now, be very consistent with the stop, whoa, and tug.

- **Match the pressure on the halter with the amount of resistance.** If your equine partner slowly drifts to a stop alongside you, then you only need a little tug on the halter to remind her that a quicker stop is expected. If, however, your horse gleefully ignores you, then use a sharp tug on the chain and a firmer verbal directive.

- **Use a fence, barn wall, or railing to keep the hindquarters in line.** Some horses, usually the pushy or spoiled ones, try to walk around their human partner by swinging their hindquarters away. Walking with a fence or wall immediately to the horse's right prevents this. Just be sure the fence is not barbed wire and the wall is free of debris. If your partner does try to swing her hindquarters away, you want to be sure she is not injured in the process.

- **Utilize corners.** Sharp 90-degree angles, such as paddock or arena corners, can be a natural barrier to forward motion. If your horse still has difficulty learning to stop, walk her close into the corner, then ask just before you reach the fence or wall. Corners make it difficult for horses to walk around you and also help eliminate the hindquarter swing.

- **Use stern eye contact to get your point across.** If your equine partner continues to walk past or around you after you have asked for the stop, repeat the sequence with firmer cues and add stern eye contact to the mix. A staredown with a horse works exactly as it would with a child or coworker; the one on the receiving end knows you mean business.

- **Make use of your normal arm swing.** Another tool you can use in the beginning stages is to exaggerate the normal swing of your left arm. This swing occurs every time you step forward. Your left arm swings forward slightly when you step with your right foot, and vice versa. As we will discuss later, horses are very conscious of your body position in relation to theirs. If you exaggerate the rhythmic swing of your left arm at the same time you ask your partner to stop, the movement brings your arm in front and slightly to the left of your horse's nose. Generally speaking, horses stop or step away from movement, so the movement near her nose should cause her to stop. This is a step you will want to phase out fairly quickly, but it can be a useful tool until your horse gets the idea.

- **Mix it up.** Be sure to vary your stopping point each time, or your equine friend will begin to anticipate, for example, that three steps past the post you are going to ask her to stop.

- **Be patient.** The length of time you actively work with your partner on this activity depends on her age and attention span. It might be five minutes for a young or inattentive horse, or twenty-five minutes for a naturally patient horse who is trying to understand. By now you will have noted your equine partner's usual signs of boredom or stress and know when to stop the lesson. Of course, if your partner has mastered the concept, then there is no point in continuing; you can move on to the next part of the activity.

- **Stay calm and focused.** Just when you do not believe you are making any progress, your equine friend will finally begin to respond correctly, so hang in there and repeat, repeat, repeat.

ADVANCED WORK

Once your equine friend is stopping well in a small enclosure at a walk, you can move into a larger area. Larger areas are always more fun for horses—there is more to see, so your friend's attention may wander. This will be a good test of how deeply the sessions have solidified in your partner's mind, because no matter what, when you say whoa, your equine partner should stop.

You can also test your partner around other horses, in the pasture, or at a show or competitive event. The more activity that is going on around your horse, the less likely it is that she will be focused 100 percent on you. You may have to use firmer cues in these instances, or hopefully your partner has learned so well that she actually stops as soon as you do, even before you say "whoa."

Once the activity has been mastered at the walk, go back to the smaller enclosure and add trotting (or an equivalent movement if your friend is gaited) to the equation. Practice walking and stopping; then walking, trotting, and stopping. Then turn around and do it again in the other direction. Once she has it down pat in the small enclosure, try her in a big, open space. Remember to be consistent and firm. You and your equine partner may go through this entire activity of walking, trotting, and moving to open spaces in five minutes, or it may take you five sessions or even longer. Just be sure to do each step in order and to be patient. Even the most spoiled horses get it eventually.

USING HAND SIGNALS

When you two are doing well at a walk and trot in different locations, it is time to add the hand signal to your list of communication tools. The hand signal can be extra reinforcement when you need to stop your horse in a hurry, or it can create an extra moment of hesitation when you are trying to convince your partner that, yes, she really does want you to catch her in the "back forty." That slight hesitation is often enough time for you to slip a rope around her neck.

Begin by returning to your small enclosure, round pen, or paddock and turning your partner loose. Now imagine that she is a clock and her head is pointing at twelve and her tail is pointing at six. Nine o'clock is approximately the center of your horse's balance at a standstill, so you want to approach her ahead of that imaginary balance line. The equivalent of ten or eleven o'clock is perfect. Remember that horses move away from pressure, but horses also move forward and back depending on where a person stands. Stand in front of the center of balance at ten o'clock, and the horse is more likely to stop or move backward. Stand behind the center of balance at seven or eight o'clock and you can unintentionally drive your horse forward.

Approaching a horse from 10 or 11 o'clock, which is in front of the horse's center of gravity at a standstill, will cause a horse to slow or stop. Approaching from 7 or 8 o'clock (or behind the center of gravity) will drive a horse forward.

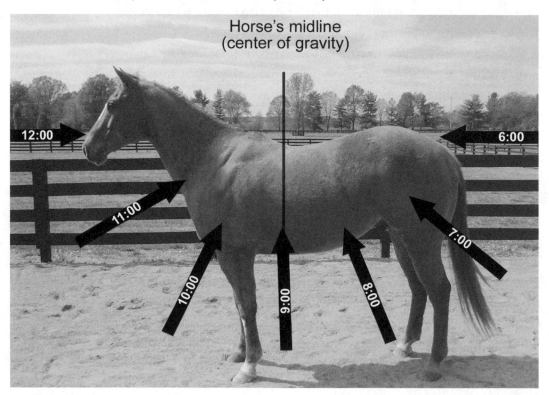

As you approach your friend from ten to twelve feet away, extend your arm and hold it as if you were stopping traffic. You can hold the halter and/or lead in the other hand. Many people prefer to hold out the left hand, which is closer to the horse's head and therefore thought to be more of a deterrent to moving forward than using the right hand. Also, because the right hand is closer to a horse's center of balance, you might inadvertently drive the horse forward by raising it. Be careful not to get too close to the twelve o'clock or six o'clock spots. Those are the blind spots and a horse could move away, if only to see better.

Your body language should be casual, yet workmanlike. You don't want to go marching up to your horse, nor do you want to walk so slowly that your horse thinks you are a pushover. It is best to maintain a pleasant expression on your face as you greet your friend by saying your horse's name, then "whoa." Saying your horse's name first gets her attention. If you say "whoa," then the horse's name, it could be that she is half-asleep and not even paying attention to you—or your words. But even a sleepy horse usually responds to his or her name.

Your speech should be friendly, but firm. Imagine yourself in your partner's shoes as you come across the pasture to her. If you shout at her, she may think there is a good reason you are shouting and decide she should get out of there. Remember that a horse's first instinctive response is to run from danger. If you are shouting, something must be wrong. On the other hand, if you have a pushy horse who is not really in the mood to go to work, if your voice is not commanding enough to get her attention, she may either turn away from you or wander off.

While you are in the small enclosure, practice the appropriate body language and tone of voice for

Recognizing Body Language

This is a good time to pay attention to your equine partner's reactions. What signals does she give when she ignores you? Does she turn her left ear sideways, raise her nose, or turn her head away from you? Does her tail swish? Does she refuse to make eye contact with you? Understanding your friend's body language at the beginning of a problem can help keep the situation from turning into an all-out battle. You may be able to distract her by doing something else for a while and then returning to the activity, or you may be able to give her extra reassurance or firmer cues. Just like people, different horses have different quirks, and it is up to you to find out what your partner is saying.

Also be sure to recognize the body language your horse uses when she begins to listen, and to understand her signals when she wants to do well. In addition to the licking and chewing most horses do in such situations, horses also give other cues, such as a lowered head. Your equine partner may blow softly through her nose, visibly relax, or demonstrate a much softer eye. Knowing when your partner is beginning to understand and cooperate is important, so that you do not make her angry or confused by giving stronger cues than she needs at that time.

your horse. At Saddle Up!, Nomo is both sensitive and hard to catch, so the approach must be right on target. Nomo must respect the person approaching, and the human partner must use a more casual posture and tone of voice. If any of those items are a little off, Nomo will gladly run circles around the person. Nacho and Valentino, on the other hand, are both very curious and will trot across a pasture to greet a visitor.

Do I still use hand signals with Nacho, who is so easily caught? Yes, because it is a reinforcement of the "whoa" directive that may be needed if he becomes hung up in a longe line, or if he becomes frightened in another type of emergency situation. For that reason, it is a good idea to use the gesture any time you stop your horse from the ground, with the exception of when you are leading him. Then, on the off chance you ever really need the gesture, it could save you or your equine partner from injury.

Once your partner is responding well in a small enclosure, try it in a larger area, such as a pasture, or a large enclosed arena. As with any other activity, remember that the bigger the area, the bigger the possibility of distraction. And depending on the nature of your gentle partner, it may seem like overkill—until the unexpected happens and you need her to stop.

Will every horse let herself be caught using this method? No, but it will increase your chances on a hard-to-catch horse, and it is a foundation for the longeing, long lining, and driving activities that you will be doing very soon.

RESULTS!

By the end of this activity, your equine partner will show you more respect, listen more closely, and stop whenever and wherever you ask. Additionally, you are noticing more about your partner's language, moods, and quirks. And those of you with horses who have sensitive body parts are finally ready to fully desensitize those areas.

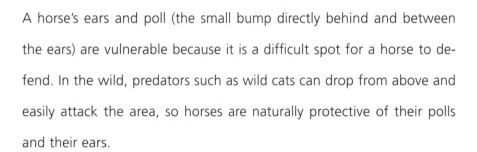

THE EARS HAVE IT

A horse's ears and poll (the small bump directly behind and between the ears) are vulnerable because it is a difficult spot for a horse to defend. In the wild, predators such as wild cats can drop from above and easily attack the area, so horses are naturally protective of their polls and their ears.

When humans came into the picture thousands of years ago, horses had to learn to trust people enough for a bridle or halter, the top of which rests just behind the poll, to be slipped over their ears. Accepting a halter is one of the first lessons every horse learns. But in the process, the horse's ears are often pulled, bumped, or bent, and the horse again learns he needs to be careful of the area. As with humans' ears, it is not necessarily painful to have the ear bent, but it is annoying and can become painful if done aggressively.

As a horse progresses in his relationship with humans, the idea of needing to protect his ears is constantly reinforced. Every time an ear is grabbed to clip the hair inside it for a horse show or event, every time an ear is twisted to restrain the horse for veterinary treatment, every time humans fumble around when haltering or bridling a horse, the horse is taught that he needs to protect his ears.

So, it's not surprising that many horses throw up their heads when their human partners approach with halter in hand. What is surprising is that *every* horse does not throw up his head in an attempt to avoid the upcoming ear-bumping session.

As your horse's partner, you first have to understand that his ears and the nearby poll are vulnerable, and make a point to treat this area gently in future dealings with him. This avoids aggravating any behavior concerning your friend's ears from this point on. But what about all the times you—and others—handled your partner's ears roughly in the past? There are probably several painful ear experiences in his history that you are not even aware of.

The same is true for the sensitive areas on his body that you have been ignoring. There are several possible reasons for the sensitivity.

1. Your horse may be ticklish. If this is the case, then you may not be able to completely desensitize the area, but it is good to know for future reference.

2. The horse may have hidden scar tissue or even internal scar tissue from an old injury that makes certain kinds of touch painful. You can help this by massaging the area. You can't completely fix the scar, but you may be able to improve sensitivity to it.

3. The most common possibility is that your equine friend associates touching that area with a scary or painful incident in his life. A tree branch may have struck his side during a storm, or a girth may have been too tight on a trail ride and created a painful bruise or sore.

There are an endless number of possibilities. Even though these are traumatic issues, you have a good chance of helping your partner completely overcome them.

Think of it this way. If you have ever been in a car that rear-ended a vehicle in front of it, you might get nervous anytime a car in which you are riding gets too close to the one ahead. It may even take you some time to feel comfortable riding in a car at all. Your partner is the same way. If he has had a bad experience with his ears or another part of his body, it will take him more time to work through this problem than a horse whose body has never been manhandled.

This is also true for the instinctive fear every horse has regarding his poll. If a horse has ever reared and hit his poll on a low ceiling, or gotten cast in a stall and bumped his poll, he will be more sensitive to having objects near the area than a horse who has not had those experiences. Unfortunately, we often do not know the full history of the horses in our care, so it can be difficult to determine which scenario applies to your friend.

Regardless, your partner will never truly be your partner until he trusts you with these sensitive and vulnerable areas. By desensitizing the ears, poll, and other overly sensitive areas, you are helping your horse build a bond of trust with you. He will learn to relax when his ears are being handled, and this will build confidence in other areas of your relationship, both on the ground and mounted.

START WITH THE EARS

To begin with your partner's ears and poll, you will only need a few objects: a halter, lead rope, pom-pom, plastic grocery bag, and some bells. Different colors of pom-poms and plastic bags, and other bells that produce a variety of sounds, will be added later. If, through your earlier desensitization work, you have found that your equine friend is more comfortable with certain colors, by all means, begin with those.

First put your horse in a small enclosure such as a stall, round pen, or small paddock; he should only be wearing a halter and lead. Nylon or leather halters are preferable, as they have a wider strap than rope halters. The wide strap will help anchor the pom-pom you will slip under the headpiece of the halter. I also like the end of the halter's headpiece strap to remain untucked, using only the top part of the buckle. That way, in the unlikely event you need to remove the halter or pom-pom in a hurry, you can undo the buckle more quickly.

Your partner should already be familiar with the pom-pom, as it is one of the objects you used to desensitize his body in Chapter Three, so he should not be afraid when you approach him with it. Let him see and smell the pom-pom, and then reintroduce it to him by lightly and rhythmically tossing it along his sides, back, and legs. Be sure to use your voice to tell your partner how wonderfully he is doing and how proud you are of him, and to use your pleasant face and casual body posture. If your partner becomes startled, or flinches after the first few minutes, go back to Chapter Three and spend as much time going over that process as needed. It shouldn't take more than a session or two.

Most likely, your horse will stand quietly as you move the pom-pom all over both sides of his body. Without any fuss, bring the pom-pom up to his face and tuck the flat end under the halter's headpiece—between his ears—so the pom-pom's streamers are covering his forelock and forehead. It's okay if the pom-pom partially covers your partner's eyes; however if the eyes are totally covered, push the pom-pom further under the headstall so his vision is not completely obstructed. Then remove the lead rope and leave your partner alone for an hour or so.

Typical first reactions from your friend might include head tossing, dropping his head down to try to pull the pom-pom off by rubbing his head against his front legs, or walking sideways to try to get away from the pom-pom. Or, your partner may freeze in place with the idea that if he doesn't know what to do, doing nothing is a good choice.

A good choice for you at this point is to inconspicuously observe your friend from a distance, at least for the first few minutes, to be sure your partner's reactions are not stronger than anything listed above. If he is doing well, leave him on his own, pom-pom in place, for as long as you can that day. You will find the vast majority of horses become accustomed to the pom-pom in less than an hour, but it won't hurt a thing for him to wear it for a longer period of time, if that is possible. However, if your partner panics and you are observing nearby, you can quickly reach him and start the process over. If he shows extreme and repeated objection to the pom-pom, or any object, place it near or in his feed bucket for a few days. If he wants to eat, he will have to get up close and personal with whatever it is he dislikes.

This is also a good opportunity to further study your horse's behavior. Is he shaking his head in an attempt to rid himself of this new thing? Is he walking while shaking his head or is he stopped? Is he bucking, baring his teeth, or is he grazing calmly? How your friend reacts here is a good indication of how well he retained his earlier desensitization. File this information away, as it could be very useful to you in introducing new items in the future.

It can also be an indicator of how often, if at all, you may need to go back and revisit earlier desensitization activities. Many of the Saddle Up! horses, including Nacho, Nelson, Valentino, and Lady, rarely need refresher sessions. However, Nomo—and now Lucky—need the sessions more regularly. Like some people, their retention rates are not as high as the others. But over the course of several years, Nomo's refresher sessions have been reduced from weekly to monthly, which is a significant improvement.

It is important to note that while *your* horse might not be afraid of the pom-poms, other horses might. After all, it's not every day they get to see a horse wearing a pom-pom on his head. It is unfortunate, but horses, like many people, are distrustful of anyone who looks different. It is not "natural" for a horse to wear a pom-pom, therefore it is something to be afraid of. If you board at a busy stable, out of courtesy you should let others who are riding nearby or working with their horses know what you are doing.

While most horses accept the pom-pom in less than an hour, your equine partner might accept it after a few minutes. Or, it might take a few sessions. It all depends on the temperament, level of training, and past experiences of your individual partner.

Once your horse is comfortable with his new headdress, you can reverse it so the streamers are facing his neck. This allows the pom-pom to touch different parts of the horse's ears and provides variation in the rustling sounds behind the ear, where the poll lies. The first time you do this, you again should remain nearby, but out of your partner's direct line of vision. This is something each horse needs to work out for himself.

BAG IT

After your partner fully accepts the pom-pom, switch to a plastic grocery bag. Any bag will do, although I prefer to begin with one that is mostly solid in color. Repeat the entire process you went through with the pom-pom, from letting him see and smell it to gently tossing it rhythmically against his body. Even though this is a reintroduction, as you will have used a similar bag in Chapter Three, the plastic bag will have smells and sounds that are different from the pom-pom. It will also have a different feel.

In placing the plastic bag under the headpiece of a horse's halter, I have had the best results if I place it evenly, with half the bag in front of the horse's ears and half behind. Being lighter in weight, the bag does not anchor as well as the pom-pom and tends to pull out from under the headpiece unless it is evenly positioned.

While the streamers of the pom-pom lightly brushed your horse's ears and blew in the wind, a plastic bag is more solid. It doesn't move a lot when a horse moves his ears, but the sound it creates can be much louder. Again, it may take several minutes or several sessions for your partner to become comfortable with this.

Throughout this process, be sure to notice the reactions of your equine friend. Does he accept the plastic bag more readily than the pom-pom, or does the louder sound and more solid feel make him more uneasy? How long does it take him to accept the bag versus the pom-pom? Is the time significantly shorter? Are the reactions less intense and of shorter duration? If so, these are signs that your equine partner is developing more trust in you. He is also growing more confident in his own abilities. If you are not seeing these signs, do not worry; you will see them at some point during the My Horse, My Partner process. Just keep watching!

RING THE BELLS

When the pom-pom and plastic bag are old hat for your partner, it is time to reintroduce the bells. There are many kinds of bells, and before you are through with My Horse, My Partner training you will have used as many different ones as you can find. The only important characteristic for the first set of bells is that they are looped in some way. You might find a set of tinkly bells strapped to a circle of leather or plastic that can also be used as a bracelet, or sleigh bells looped around a handhold that are part of a percussion set, or you might find small individual bells and rig up something that works for you.

When you reacquaint your horse with the bells, let him see and smell them. But instead of lightly and rhythmically tossing the bells along his body, just shake the bells over his back and rump, along his sides and legs, and under his belly. Again, due to the shape and possible weight of the bells, even lightly tossing them as you did the pom-pom and plastic grocery bag could be uncomfortable. After your partner shows you he is accepting of the noise and movement of the bells, slip them through the headpiece of his halter and leave him be. It is especially important with the bells that your halter fit correctly, with several fingers' width between the bottom of the horse's cheekbone and the top of the nosepiece of the halter. If the halter is too loose, the bells may slide down toward your horse's left or right cheek. While not a bad thing in itself, the horse does not get the benefit of hearing and feeling the bells in his ear and poll area if they have slid down the halter strap.

Again, as long as your partner is reasonably quiet, leave him to explore this new object on his own.

STEP IT UP

When you know your horse is comfortable with the pom-pom in front of and in back of his ears, and with both the plastic grocery bag and the bells, it's time to step it up. First, go through the process of introducing a new pom-pom. It is amazing what a difference a new color can make to some horses. Your partner might feel great about the blue pom-pom, but introduce a white one and it's like you are starting from scratch. Pom-poms also come in a variety of sizes, so experiment with different colors and shapes.

You can also place two pom-poms under the halter's headpiece, one facing forward and one facing behind. This doubles the feel of objects blowing around your partner's ears and also doubles the sound the pom-poms make. Depending on the width and length of the streamers, and whether or not some of the streamers are made of metallic paper or plastic, the feel and sound can vary. You can even make your own pom-pom by cutting strips of plastic or newspaper and taping one end of the strips to a Popsicle stick.

The same process can be undertaken with the plastic bags. A change in color, size, or weight of a bag can make a big difference to a horse. So go through the process with as many different colors and shapes and styles of plastic bags as you can find. But, as with the pom-poms, make sure you reintroduce every object before working with it, and that your partner fully accepts each individual pom-pom or plastic bag before moving on to another.

Once your equine friend can wear a variety of pom-poms and plastic bags, it is time to introduce different sizes and sounds of bells. As with the various sizes and colors of pom-poms and bags, you may find your horse reacting positively or negatively to certain sounds. It could be that a certain tone or volume hurts his ears. Or maybe he shows his preference for one of the bells by being more engaged with you and it. Pay close attention to what your equine partner is telling you, start with sounds that do not bother him as much, and then work up to the ones that are more troublesome.

Many horses do well with color and touch, but have trouble accepting objects that make noise. If that is the case with your equine friend, know that patience is the key. Repeating the same actions over and over will eventually show your partner there is nothing to fear. It is all about making unique events routine.

PROBLEM SPOTS

Finally, you two are ready to tackle those problem areas.

Lucky is very ticklish along his sides and had a very tough time accepting any kind of desensitization along his midsection. Once I realized that the pom-pom and smaller plastic bags were tickling him and were therefore uncomfortable, I switched to feed sacks and heavy black plastic shavings bags. Even though these items were larger, they were easier for Lucky to accept because they did not tickle him. After he was comfortable accepting the larger items, we could then go back to the smaller ones. He will probably always be a little flinchy on his sides with the smaller objects, but I now understand he is not shrinking away because he is afraid, but because it tickles. Now that he is in the more advanced levels of his activities, as long as his feet do not move away from the object, he can flinch all he wants.

Working through these problem areas is really a lesson in creativity. It is also a time for you to think back about some of the behavior you have watched your equine partner exhibit to determine what specific objects cause the least reaction, and to start again with those. You may even want to go back to touching and massaging with your hands. Sometimes you have to massage an area for what seems like thousands of hours, then progress to tossing a pom-pom on the area over and over again. Sometimes, if your horse is especially nervous, you have to stand firm and ask him to stand still. This is where your "whoa" cue really comes in handy, as does the respect, confidence, and trust he has recently learned. Know that eventually the vast majority of horses accept it and you can move on.

Looking at other possibilities, Nelson, a former Western pleasure show horse, is a delicate child. He truly is a hot-house flower of a horse. If there is skin to be sunburned, an allergy to have, a bruise to get, Nelson is the horse at Saddle Up! who finds it. When he first arrived, he accepted most things very quickly, except along his girth area. Many horses become "girthy" when they are saddled improperly, too quickly, or too tightly, but Nelson hadn't been ridden recently

Valentino has become so accustomed to the pom-poms being tossed all over his body that he does not mind wearing them as a headdress.

so I ruled those causes out. I also ruled out his anticipating pain in being girthed. Nelson has a very uncomplicated personality. He is eager to please, if a little lazy, but not one who thinks ahead of himself. I went back to the hand-massaging and was surprised to find patches of tiny gnat bites in the tender folds of skin inside his elbow that had been missed earlier. Poor Nelson wasn't being girthy, he was just very uncomfortable with that area because it hurt. Once the gnat bites cleared up, he felt more comfortable being touched in that area.

So think outside the box for your problem areas. Be creative, patient, confident, and firm. You will make progress, but you will

At the walk in the round pen, Valentino keeps an ear on his human partner, ready to trot or stop on cue. The pom-poms do not bother him at all.

The Benefits of Pom-poms

The benefits of a horse wearing a pom-pom between his ears are many. First, it accustoms the horse to his ears being continually touched without him associating the idea with you. This is especially important if your equine partner does not like his ears being handled. The more your partner moves, the more the streamers of the pom-pom will brush against his ears. If there is some wind and the horse is outside, Mother Nature will take care of this for you, blowing the streamers all around the horse's head.

While not a major goal of this exercise, the action of the wind will also accustom him to see-ing, in his peripheral vision, unexpected objects blow close to him. This helps a spooky or insecure horse tremendously as he gains confidence in, and experience with, unknown objects flying near his face and poll.

In addition to pom-poms benefiting in the areas of touch and vision, there is the audible sound of rustling as your partner moves. Sound that close to a horse's ears can be a fearful thing; wearing the pom-pom will teach him not to be afraid.

most likely have to take your successes in small steps. Over the course of weeks and months, though, you will be able to look back and see just how far you have come.

RESULTS!

So, other than making your horse look really silly, what has all this accomplished? Well, by the time you both have successfully mastered the ideas in this chapter, your equine friend will allow you to place noisy, potentially scary objects on his body in the one place he can't see. There is a certain amount of trust involved in that, and the person your partner trusts is you!

Your partner also has gained confidence in himself. He is wiser—more worldly—and certainly not afraid of a little piece of plastic. As a result, an insecure horse will not lean into you as often when a situation, in his eyes, is uncertain. He also will walk more confidently beside you and not stop as often if a strange sight, such as a horse wearing an unusual headdress, appears.

The pushy or ill-mannered horse will also show improvement. After all, it is a humbling experience to have a plastic bag attached to your head. A pushy horse will respect you for getting him to accept all the different objects.

And what about you? How many other people do you know who have accomplished what you did? The fact that you had the determination and patience to get your partner to accept and feel comfortable with many unusual objects is a testament to your skill as a horse person and as your horse's partner.

You've also learned much about your partner. How does he react when uncertain? Does he freeze up, pin his ears, or look to you or other horses to help him? Does he whinny? Does your partner most prefer the pom-poms, plastic, or bells? Did he show interest in playing with any of the objects? What did he do when you removed the items? All of these questions are key to learning more about your equine friend.

Remember though, that while you are beginning to see some changes in yourself and your horse, you both still have a long way to go. If you two are ready, let's move on.

PAPER OR PLASTIC

Recently, I was a clinician at a horse fair and was given thirty minutes to help a problem horse. Of course, not much can be "fixed" in half an hour, but often I, or another clinician, can help a horse and his or her owner find the right path.

This particular horse was a beautiful nine-year-old Morgan gelding who had just retired from the show ring. His new owner wanted to take lessons on him, and use him for pleasure riding. The problem was that this horse, who had won many ribbons at national-caliber events, had never experienced much outside of the show ring. Hence, he spooked whenever he saw a plastic bag, an umbrella, a windbreaker, a baby stroller, leaves blowing off the trees, or even a red mounting block. This behavior was obviously a problem to his owner, who needed some guidance.

By the end of the thirty-minute session we had quickly covered the hands-on activity. As a clinician, I was not allowed to take anything into the arena for this session, so I was without my trusty stash of pom-poms for desensitization work, but my down vest worked almost as well. We did a short respect session with halter and lead that asked the horse for the immediate and correct response to walk, trot, turn, and "whoa," and at the very end I was able to lift the scary red mounting block up onto the gelding's back and lead him around the arena.

I am not a big fan of quick fixes or "miracle sessions" done at clinics. The point of this story is that just a little effort can go a long way toward making your equine partner respectful of you, and at ease with whatever might come across his path.

INTRODUCING THE FRIENDLY WHIP

By now both you and your equine friend should be very comfortable with all of the earlier activities. She should let you touch her all over, stand quietly for desensitization with a variety of objects, and respect the word "whoa." You will have found her preferences and dislikes; recognize her signs of distress, anger, and acceptance; and have begun bonding on an entirely new level.

You may also have found, for example, that while your equine partner tolerates clear plastic, she does not like it. And that's okay. You cannot force a horse to like something any more than you can force your child to enjoy broccoli or your spouse to have fun with your parents. You can, however, expect that each family member—and your partner—will do his or her best.

It is now time to add another component to the mix by introducing items attached to a longe or dressage whip, fishing pole, or other stick-type tool. Not only does this activity combine two objects (up to now your equine partner has only been processing one item at a time), it introduces something that many horses fear: a whip. Essentially, a whip is an extension of your arm. It is a training aid, not a tool for punishment. Too many people brandishing a whip improperly have turned it into a four-letter word, but used properly, your horse should not fear a whip any more than he or she would fear your arm. Of course, all horses should respect both. The following activity will decrease any fear your equine friend has surrounding a whip, and increase her respect for it, and you.

Just like the overhand arm movement, a whip is a big threat to a horse who has ever been on the receiving end of its lash. With that in mind, your equine partner may be more uncomfortable to begin with. When you desensitize your friend to a whip, do just as you have with other desensitization activities: begin in a paddock or round pen with pleasant facial expressions, a conversational voice, and relaxed body posture. Introduce the whip by letting your horse smell it, and then casually rub it over her body—on both sides—as you talk to her. She should remember the earlier desensitization work, so you may be surprised at how quickly she accepts this.

Now that you both are attuned to the "whoa" cue, you can use it to correct any movement your partner might make. And if you work at a pace your horse is comfortable with, you may not need to ask for a whoa at all. By this point, your equine friend should trust you enough to know that you are not going to hurt her, and that trust should extend to quicker acceptance of any new concept, including this one.

If your horse has had the unfortunate experience of being abused by someone using a whip, this activity may take a little longer than the others. Know that you are doing a good thing by helping your partner overcome her fear; and your posture, face, and voice will reassure her just as much as the desensitization activity.

Once your equine friend has accepted the rubbing of the whip, next move to slow and casual underhand movements followed by sidearm movements, bringing your arm slowly back, then toward your friend. Begin by stopping the whip a foot or so from your horse, but once she relaxes you can bring the whip closer and closer, eventually ending by softly touching your equine partner with its tip. As she increasingly accepts this process, you can make your sidearm movements faster, but never land the whip harder on your partner's body than a soft touch.

Again, as you go through the motions, watch for your friend's individual signs of fear, anger, or acceptance, and adjust your session accordingly. Once your partner has reached acceptance, indicated by relaxed ears and body, soft eye, low head, quiet tail, and licking or chewing motions with her mouth, you can move on. But, if your horse is reluctant to accept this—or any other process—slow down, take a step back, and repeat, repeat, repeat until acceptance occurs. You have to make the unique routine, and sometimes that takes time.

The next step is to repeat the activity with overhand movements. You already know that this is one of the most threatening gestures you can make toward a horse, so realize how much implicit trust your equine partner has in you to accept this. Before moving on, be sure your friend is fully accepting of all the arm movements we have discussed from both sides and at different speeds.

The final element is to stand at your partner's head, and face her hip with the lead rope in your left hand and the whip in your right. This places you in a position to see all of your equine partner's body, so you can better gauge her reactions. You can then raise your right hand over your head, keeping your elbow straight, and slowly lower your arm, whip in hand, so the whip almost touches the ground in front of you. Start slowly, and as your horse becomes more and more comfortable, work up to faster and faster arm speeds.

Beginning with the time you first picked up the whip to rub it over your equine friend's body, the entire process may take five minutes, or five weeks. Patience is the key, so keep doing it over and over again at whatever level your partner is comfortable. Slowly take it up a few notches until she tells you she is uncomfortable, then back down slightly. By doing this, you are slowly raising the bar on your horse's comfort level, and over time, you will be amazed at what you both have accomplished.

YOUR HORSE IS STILL A HORSE

By now it should be evident that horses do not think like humans. Humans nod, smile, and shake hands to indicate acceptance, while horses drop their heads and smack their lips. While humans understand that an umbrella is still an umbrella no matter the color, shape, style, or location, horses think of each of those umbrellas as separate things. To a horse, a closed blue umbrella leaning against a stall is not at all the same as an open green and white striped umbrella being carried by a little girl.

That's why it is important to introduce as many different objects to your partner as possible. Eventually, even though your horse will always think like a horse, some of the objects may connect in your equine friend's brain and she will at some point realize that a white soccer ball in her stall and an orange basketball in the arena really are not so different after all.

Some of the things your partner might see throughout her lifetime could be very odd: a parade float, a hot-air balloon, a bicycle built for two, a cross-country skier, a group of motorcyclists. Nothing can prepare your horse for every eventuality, but the next part of this activity will help lessen the effects of the unexpected.

Even though Valentino has been through a great deal of desensitization, a very large red and yellow stagecoach that was roped off by orange crime-scene tape recently startled him. We were at a horse fair for a demonstration, and were leading the Saddle Up! horses across the grounds when we came around a corner, and there it was. Even though Nacho, Nelson, and the rest of the horses went by the stage-coach without batting an eye, Valentino was obviously terrified. He planted his feet, threw up his head and stared at this monstrosity with bug eyes as he visibly shook.

What interested me most, though, was what Valentino did not do. He did not try to run away, proving that his training overcame his natural instinct to flee. He also did not breathe large snorts of air through his nose, a classic sign that a horse is uncertain. Instead, Valentino just froze. During the event, I was very conscious of the trust Valentino had placed in me by choosing to stay even when he was so frightened he was shaking. In his mind, he was trusting me with his life. I couldn't help but think how many people I would trust with my own life and the list was not very long. I was, and am, honored to be included on Valentino's list.

I spent a few moments talking to Valentino before I asked him to walk by the stagecoach. I wanted to see signs that he was relaxing before I asked him to move forward. Only when he lowered his head a fraction, when his ears flicked back and forth, when he began to breathe, and his muscles stopped twitching, did I ask him to move on. He accompanied me quite willingly as he tiptoed past the colorful stagecoach. He could have bolted past me. He could have jumped into me or on top of me, or whirled around to face the big scary thing, but he did none of those things. Valentino just carefully walked by.

Given the option, I certainly would rather have a horse who just stops when frightened, rather than one who whirls around to run away, or one who jumps ten steps sideways. Will Valentino ever do those things? Maybe. But due to his training, it will be far less often than a horse who has not been through extensive desensitizing activities.

TOOLKIT COMBINATIONS

Now that your equine partner has accepted the whip by itself, you can tie an object to it that your friend is already familiar with, such as a bag or pom-pom. Most dressage whips or other crops have a little string on the end, or a loop of leather. Each provides a good place to tie. I prefer the dressage-length whip to start with, but you can use a shorter crop if you do not have a dressage whip available. Save the longe whips for later. Additionally, most of the commercial "training sticks" do not have the flex or bend that is perfect for this activity, so stay with whips, if at all possible.

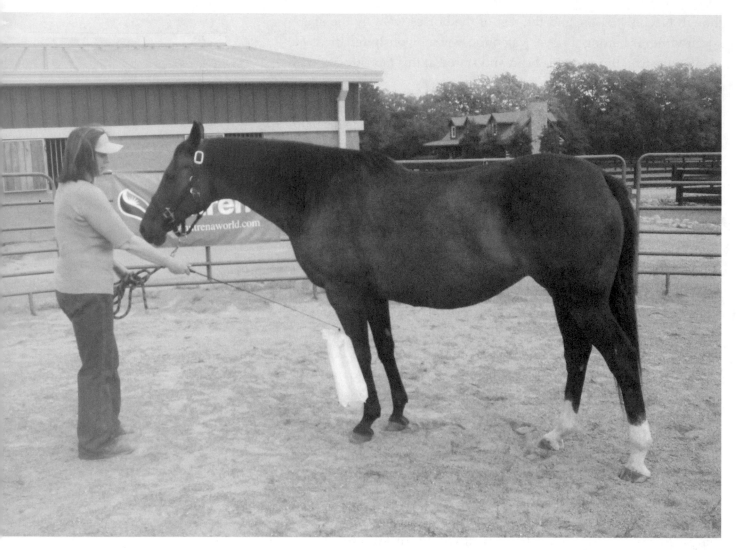

Nomo is not completely happy, but she is quiet around the whip and bag combination.

By introducing two elements your horse is already familiar with, you have a better chance that your friend will quickly grasp the concept that "here is another very strange new thing, but it won't hurt me," than if you introduce the whip with a ball she has never seen before tied to it. It also helps if the second object you choose is one she has shown a preference for, such as a particular red bag or a blue washcloth. Remember that just because your equine friend is comfortable with a whip and a white plastic bag, she will not necessarily think of the two objects together as something she has already seen. To her, it will be brand new.

Plus, there is the added factor that the object at the end of the whip is not directly attached to your hand. A plastic bag attached to and controlled by your hand might be safe, according to your partner. But a plastic bag at the end of a whip moves differently than one controlled directly by your hand, so it may be considered a brand new scary object.

In your small, enclosed area, rub the whip and the object over your horse's body until your equine friend shows you she is relaxed and accepting. Then stand a few feet away from your partner, as you did when you were raising the whip over your head and bringing it down to the floor. With the lead rope in your left hand, and the whip with bag or pom-pom tied to it in your right, gently raise and lower the whip/bag combination in a slow rhythm. Remember that rhythms relax your equine partner and help her anticipate when the next sound or movement will come. You can also talk conversationally to your friend and reassure her with your facial expressions and body posture.

When your equine partner accepts the slow, rhythmic movement from both sides, you can begin bringing the slow movements closer and closer to her body. When you finally touch your horse with it, remember where her ticklish spots are and, at least to begin with, stay away from those areas. It is hard for anyone to stay focused when being tickled. You will progress much as before, rubbing the object on the end of the whip all over your equine partner's body from both sides, correcting her when she moves too much, and using your voice, body, and face to reassure her. Underhand movements are followed by sidearm movements, which are followed by overhand movements. Remember that you are never going to do more than touch your partner's body with the objects. If she seems ticklish with the touch, you can try landing the object just a little bit harder, but never so hard that it is in any way uncomfortable.

Also know that the various objects at the end of the whip have different weights. A washcloth lands more heavily than a plastic bag, so adjust your arm movements accordingly, so you do not land the object on your partner too hard. Keep in mind that many horses have a preconceived idea of a whip as a tool that is used for punishment, so you do not want to do anything that reinforces that concept.

MIX IT UP

When your friend has told you she is very comfortable with the first object tied to the whip, try another that you have already introduced.

Maybe it is a stuffed animal, a colorful slinky, a foam rubber ball, or a pink paisley scarf. After exhausting use of all the known items, you can be as creative as you like. If you can tie it to the end of a dressage or similar whip, and if it is something that will not hurt your equine partner in any way, then go for it. Repeat, repeat, repeat the process of rubbing, rhythmic movement, and touching with as many objects as you can find, one at a time, until your partner has accepted them all.

LONGE WHIP

Once you have exhausted the possibilities for dressage whip/object combinations, try moving up to a longe whip. Longe whips are much

Different Reactions

Even if your partner seems like she is accepting everything with no problems, it is important to go through as many objects as you can find. At Saddle Up! everyone thought Nelson was oblivious to all outside stimuli. He accepted all the unusual tools and objects used in therapeutic riding and never batted an eye. Then one day he took a look at a new polo mallet an instructor wanted to use in a lesson and jumped two feet in the air.

Nelson's unexpected reaction illustrates how important it is to regularly add new items to your toolkit. Of course, the new objects only help if you take time to introduce them properly to your equine partner. But as you are seeing, as you go through this process your equine friend will accept most new things far more quickly than she did before, so it won't always be quite so time consuming.

Depending on your horse's past experiences, you may discover that she absolutely will not tolerate an item, such as orange plastic. You can go through the desensitization exercises over and over and she still is not comfortable. It is probable, then, that your friend had a traumatic experience involving orange plastic, and she may never accept it. To her, it will forever be imprinted in her mind that this is a frightful thing. Keep reassuring her, feed her on top of the scary color, have it hanging in her stall, and maybe the fear will lessen over time. If not, at least you know one of her triggers and can be on the lookout for orange plastic as you continue to be around and enjoy your equine friend.

On the other hand, if you have a playful horse, like Nacho, it is best to keep the sessions away from your friend's face. If your partner is busy trying to grab an object with her teeth or trying to stomp on it with her front feet, she cannot be aware that it makes a rustling noise as it flies through the air, or recognize the feel when it lands on her back, so she is not really being desensitized to the object. There is room for play, but in a later activity.

Fishing is more Nomo's style. Here she watches intently as I raise and lower a white ball tied to the end of a longe whip. Note the lead rope, which is correctly held in both hands, and in a figure eight.

longer and allow you to drag an object in front of a horse, into and out of her line of vision. You can toss a paper bag tied to the end of a longe whip completely over your horse's back and let it land on the ground on the opposite side, or run it across the front of her rear hooves, or up her hocks.

Working with a longe whip takes a little practice, so if this is new for you, try it a few times without your partner in sight. Only when you have excellent control of the whip should you bring your equine friend into the mix. If you do not have a longe whip, an old cane fishing pole works well, or even a rod and reel.

This time, due to the length of the whip or pole, you can drag and pull the tied object around, over, and under your equine partner. Remember to go at your partner's pace, rather than at your pace. Watch her closely, and she will tell you when she is ready for more, or when you need to backtrack and go more slowly.

I find that introducing a variety of new things also keeps my equine friends mentally sharp. Streamers, flags, and other such objects especially intrigue Nomo. She is very alert when they are used around

Nomo is uneasy as a streamer flutters toward her. She has picked up a hoof in preparation for moving away, but does so slowly before stopping to inspect the streamer further. Nomo feels more comfortable with this object without the restraint of the lead rope as she can explore at her own pace without the streamer being forced upon her.

her, but she rarely steps away. You can see the wheels of her mind turning as she processes the object and what it means to her safety. Nacho, on the other hand, tries to grab or chase the streamer as it flies through the air, and Lady looks at me as if I am the village idiot. Each reaction, while very different, provides mental stimulation that shakes up daily boredom and gives our equine friends something new to think about.

Once you have pushed, pulled, and dragged all the balls, kids' toys, streamers, flags, bags, stuffed animals, and towels that you can find, you could try a small, green, leafy branch, or a piece of a dried shrub. Just be sure to remove any sharp points or thorns. Natural elements move and smell differently than those that are man-made, so there is the added possibility of picking up the scent of a possum, squirrel, or raccoon in the leaves or branches.

RESULTS!

Did you ever think you could snap a whip mere inches from your partner's body and not have her move a muscle? Or pull a slinky past her hind legs, or toss a fishing line with a stuffed animal over her back? The trust and confidence you each have individually, and as a team, is rapidly growing. And, you are developing an instinctive feel for the messages your horse is sending.

LEADING

When I was in 4-H, a local trainer suggested I practice my showmanship at halter skills without the halter. How in the world, I wondered, was that going to work? The precision needed to get a horse to walk and trot perfectly straight lines, stop square, turn on a dime, and back was difficult enough. How could it possibly be accomplished without a halter or lead rope? The trainer went on to explain that if my horse was well trained and respectful, that he didn't really need a halter. He should follow me wherever I wanted, and as fast or as slow as I needed.

When I tried the exercise I was amazed in two ways. I was first pleasantly surprised at how much of the pattern work my horse and I could accomplish without the halter and lead. But second, I realized how much further my "perfectly trained" horse and I had to go. Until that moment, I really believed my horse knew how to lead, and that I knew how to lead him.

Leading is a basic function of the horse/human partnership. It is also, possibly, the most overlooked part of the training process. When a horse leads properly, his ears should be next to his leader's shoulder. He should not be dancing sideways, jumping ahead, or even worse, lagging behind.

The more I pull Lady, the more she drags behind. This puts unneeded pressure on her neck and back, and can cause soreness.

Leading properly is not only a sign of trust and respect; it is a safety issue. If a horse is jigging sideways, swinging his hindquarters away from his leader, the leader is then positioned in front of the horse. If the horse jumped forward, he could knock his leader to the ground. And, if a leader is too far in front of a lagging horse, the leader can more easily be bitten by the horse, or pushed out of the way as the horse moves forward. If a horse is too far ahead of the leader, the leader does not have any leverage to control the horse if he decides to walk off in another direction. The horse can also use his shoulder to bump the leader out of his way.

Improper leading can also bring about soreness in a horse, especially if your equine friend is one who has to be pulled along. Picture this: as you pull on the lead rope to encourage your horse to move faster, your energy-challenged equine friend decides to stretch his neck forward, rather than move faster. As he stretches his neck, his nose tilts up, his neck flattens, and his back hollows out. Additionally, his back legs end up behind him, rather than underneath him. Soon, rather than a square, balanced horse, your equine partner becomes so long and unbalanced that stress is put across his entire topline, causing soreness from poll to tail. Once your friend becomes sore, he can become cranky and unwilling to perform the most routine tasks, and he can take weeks to heal.

It surprises me that most of the horses and leaders I see at my clinics have never been taught to lead correctly. The good news is that teaching your equine partner to lead well is relatively easy, once a good foundation is in place. And if your equine friend has accepted the earlier My Horse, My Partner activities (especially learning to respect both you and the whoa cue), your foundation is already there.

LEADING ASSESSMENT

First, begin with a leading assessment at both the walk and trot. Does your partner lag behind? Does he try to bite you when trotting? Does he lead as well from the right side as he does from the left? Does he stop and turn easily? At Saddle Up! each of the horses leads differently, and how they lead reflects each horse's personality. Lucky is slow to start and tends to drop behind his leader. Nomo is more energetic and sometimes has to be encouraged to fall back. Nacho will tug on his leader's clothing if he thinks he can get away with it. Know that while each horse's personality is vastly different, every horse can learn perfect leading manners.

Once you have an idea of your equine partner's leading strengths and weaknesses, you can develop a plan to improve leading safety, performance, and ease.

THE BASICS

Begin by being sure your halter fits correctly, with the nosepiece falling several fingers' width below your partner's cheekbones, with the noseband loose enough to stick all your fingers through, but not too loose. Hold your lead rope with the hand that is closest to your horse, eight to ten inches from the halter. Grasp the end of the rope in your other hand in a figure eight, and never coil or loop it around your hand. If your partner suddenly pulled away, it could tighten and permanently injure your hand. If your lead rope is a little shorter, you can let the end dangle, as long as it does not reach below your knees. Any longer and there is the possibility of tripping over the rope, or of it wrapping itself around your legs.

To me, leading horses is similar to the story of Goldilocks and the three bears. One horse will walk too far in front of you, one will be too far behind you, and one will lead just right. If your equine partner is one who, like Nomo, likes to be in front, correct response to "whoa" is extra important. Every time your partner gets too far in front of you,

Lady is much happier when she leads correctly. Using a dressage whip behind you, as an extension of your arm, can help teach your equine partner to lead properly.

just ask him to stop and stand. Then ask him to move forward, but as soon as he gets too far in front, stop and stand again. You may only get two or three steps before you have to ask for the halt, but before too long, your friend will understand that whenever he gets ahead of you he is going to have to stop. In due course he will begin to automatically check his position and keep himself aligned with you.

If your horse does not listen or becomes impatient, you may have to go back and revisit the "whoa" activities in Chapter Four. Or, try working with a lead chain for a few sessions.

If your equine friend is of the slower variety, a dressage whip in your outside hand effectively lengthens your reach so you can tap your friend behind his center of gravity. Remember that at a walk, your partner's center of gravity is just behind the withers. To get him to move forward, he will need to receive a tap behind that center point. Every time he falls back, reach behind you and give him a light tap on his flank to remind him to walk with you, rather than behind you.

You will have to experiment with the amount of pressure needed to get your equine partner to respond. Some horses will immediately begin walking correctly beside you if you are just holding a dressage whip. Others need a light tap a time or two, while some need a slightly stronger reminder. Eventually, of course, your partner will not need any reminder, as you will have helped him develop the good habit of walking with his ears next to your shoulder.

STOPPING

As you have already worked extensively on the correct response to "whoa," your friend should stop immediately with a verbal cue. A more advanced exercise is to ask your equine partner to stop just by stopping yourself. All you have to do is very purposefully stop walking. If he does not respond, try again. This time stop walking, and then pull back on the halter, being sure to release the pressure as soon as he stops. Or you can stop walking, pull back, and say whoa, in that specific order. Eventually he will understand that as soon as you stop, he is to stop also.

The other scenario is when your partner decides to stop on his own. Sometimes when leading a horse toward a barn he suddenly realizes it is time to go to work and comes to a screeching halt. Rather than pull on a horse's topline, a good technique is to ask the horse to take a few steps to the left, and then to the right. Alternate left and right a few times and by the time you resume forward motion toward the barn, he will have forgotten all about stopping.

This zigzag process may have to be repeated a few times, but it eventually will get you where you want to go. Be sure to point your face and body in the direction you want to go, and to keep your eyes away from your partner's. Making eye contact in such a situation can seem like a challenge to your equine friend, and will just reinforce his will to stop.

TROTTING

Just as your equine partner should slow or stop exactly when you do, he should also move faster along with you. If you walk faster or begin to jog, he should jog alongside you. If he doesn't understand the process, or is a little lazy, you can add the word "trot" to your physical jogging cue. At first, the verbal cue may not be enough to get his attention, so a few light taps with the dressage whip may be needed. Your horse will probably remember the earlier walking sessions, so just carrying it may be enough incentive for him to respond correctly. If not, just repeat the reaching back you did to encourage him to walk with you.

If your equine friend becomes a little excited about trotting with you and tries to leave you in the dust, try trotting for just a few steps, and when he moves ahead of you ask him to transition down to the walk, or even to stop. Before long, he will understand that as soon as he moves ahead of you, the fun is over and he will have to stop. Eventually, he will realize that it is easier to trot along nicely.

It is also very important to gauge the strength of the cue needed for your equine partner. Saddle Up! has an ancient Shetland pony by the name of King Bee. Bee is well into his thirties and only has one serviceable tooth left in his mouth, but all you have to do to get him to trot is to start walking faster. If you break into a jog, Bee is likely to jump into

Lady prefers to walk, but here she keeps up well at the trot.

a canter. Having a horse like King Bee—versus one like Nelson, who clearly would rather take a nap—means the intensity of your cue is vastly different. Ask too strongly and one partner will unintentionally leave you behind. But if you are not clear or firm enough with another horse, you will end up pulling on his neck and creating a sore topline.

TURNING

I see many horses who follow their leader very well along a straight path, but who bump their shoulder into their leader's hip, or even step on the leader's toes when they are asked to make a left or right turn. Turning should not be that difficult. If you turn your partner's head away from you, he should turn smoothly to the right. If you pull his head toward you and walk to the left, he should come right on along.

Leading your partner in circles, serpentines, or figure eights can be excellent practice and can also show which direction your friend prefers to travel. If your horse is older he will probably have more muscle on one side of his body than the other. This is due to years of traveling a particular way and can cause soreness. If this is the case, additional work may be needed turning to the left or to the right.

Just as people are naturally left- or right-handed, a young horse will show a natural preference toward one side or the other. Valentino definitely prefers to travel to the left and has never been completely comfortable working to the right. It is harder for him to pick up his right lead than the left, and he has more difficulty bending his body in that direction. On his own in the pasture, Valentino will pick up the left lead, rather than the right, nine times out of ten. He is willing, but physically he has to work harder at it.

If you have a strong-willed partner who actively resists you, turning can be a great exercise in dominance. If you are leading your partner from the left and turn to the right, you are turning into the horse, and because you are essentially pushing yourself into his space, your equine friend recognizes you as the dominant, or alpha, partner. That's why, whenever I have the choice, I always turn toward the horse. It is a non-verbal reminder of who is in charge.

If your horse disrespects you by ignoring your turning cues, stop and give a direct stare into his eye. In horse language, a direct stare is a challenge or confrontation and this lets your horse know you mean business. Then, repeat the request using firm body language and words with periods or exclamation points on the end. If you are still being ignored, a short session on leading, stopping, and turning with the lead chain will help.

LEADING FROM THE "WRONG" SIDE

Just as it was important to desensitize your equine friend from both sides, so is it important that your partner lead equally well from both sides. If your friend ever gets in a bind and has to be led from the right, you want him to respond to you correctly.

Years ago a rainstorm washed away a huge chunk of earth from a narrow trail that I regularly rode. The wash created a steep drop on the right side of the trail, which wasn't something I wanted to travel next to while still mounted. My little Appaloosa mare, Snoqualmie, instinctively knew the inside of the trail, which was closely bordered by boulders and trees, was safer, and she hugged the inside edge. But when I tried to lead her from the left, I found that to keep to the safer inside of the trail, Snoqualmie had to position herself behind me. Afraid that she would try to leap over me, I moved to the right side and led her along the edge of the trail. Snoqualmie's natural inclination to stay away from the crumbly edge allowed her the firmer ground on the inside, and my considerably lighter weight was safer than she was on the outer edge.

You never know when you will encounter such a situation, so it is important that both you and your equine partner learn to be comfortable with leading on both sides. Working on both left and right will also help your horse overcome the one-sidedness that is common to all horses. And, because horses are almost always handled from the left, it is often awkward for the human partner to work from the right side. To lead from the right you have to switch hands, keeping your left hand closer to the halter. Your equine friend, whose left and right sides of his brain do not really connect, has to learn all over again to lead properly. He will have to get used to seeing you monocularly out of his right eye, rather than his left, and to smell and hear you on the right, when he normally experiences this from the left.

Depending on how ambidextrous you are, leading your horse from the right side may take a little practice. At first he may be confused and not want to move forward, and you may be quite awkward

Biting Cures

Under the right circumstances, any horse can bite. Biting is a way for a horse to show his human partner that he is angry, in pain, frightened, resentful, or even playful. That said, biting is dangerous and not acceptable. If you have an equine partner who tends to bite there are several actions you can take to discourage the behavior.

First, stop feeding your horse from your hand. Even though he may not bite during feeding, this is a horse who needs to have his mouth and nose left alone as much as possible. Remember that a horse cannot see your hand when it is at the end of his nose. If you feed treats by hand to your equine friend, he is going to associate the treat not only with the smell of the apples, molasses, oats, or carrots, but also with the smell of your hand. Consequently, when you lead your horse with your hand near his mouth, he is getting a whiff of your hand and thinking, "treat, treat, treat!"

While you don't want to feed a biter from your hand or play with his nose, there are also some proactive steps you can take to further discourage the behavior. My favorite is the rope twirl. While it takes some practice, it is very effective and only corrects the horse when he makes the mistake of invading your space with his teeth bared.

The idea is to twirl the end of a lead rope in a clockwise direction as you lead your equine partner. If he turns in to bite, the end of the lead rope will whop his nose. If he behaves correctly, he will not be touched. It is important to twirl the last twelve inches or so of the lead in a clockwise direction, so the end of the lead will come down on top of the horse's nose, rather than up under the horse's chin. If the rope hits him under the chin, it will cause him to throw his head up. Then, every time he thinks about biting, he will jerk his head, which can become very annoying.

The technique, while simple, does require a little practice for most people. Start without

Horses can bite if they are sore, spoiled, or fearful. To prevent the occasional nip, twirl the end of the lead rope clockwise. If a horse turns her nose in to bite, the rope will catch her on top of her nose.

your equine partner by holding a lead rope in your left hand (about a foot from the end), and practice gently twirling the end of the lead in a clockwise direction. When you can vary the speed and intensity with some regularity, practice twirling while walking and jogging. Remember only to twirl clockwise.

When you feel competent, attach the snap end of the lead rope to the ring under your horse's halter and face forward as if you were going to ask your horse to walk. Slowly begin twirling the end of the lead and keep doing so until your equine friend is calm and relaxed with the process. Only then should you ask your friend to move forward. Keep twirling at a walk, and then at a trot. If your partner acts as if he is going to bite, twirl faster. If you make contact, be prepared for your horse to stop, or to jerk his head away. This is a good time to practice a stern facial expression and body posture as you stop, and look directly into your horse's eye. Remember that in horse language, a direct stare is a challenge. This time, you are telling your partner that biting is not acceptable and are challenging him to accept that understanding.

After a few moments, relax your face and body and ask your horse to walk on. Repeat the walking and twirling (and trotting and twirling) until your partner stops the biting behavior. Remember, too, that biting can be a habit, and that habits are hard to break. Even though your equine partner may remember not to bite, the remembering part may come a split second after the action has started. Just like trying to stop

biting your fingernails, your intentions are good, but you automatically do it anyway. Your equine friend may struggle with the same thing for a while, so be patient. You may have to continue the twirling for weeks, or even longer.

Eventually you should get to the point that the outward movement of your left arm will serve as a good reminder to your partner. Just bring your left arm a few inches away from your body, so your equine friend can see the end of the lead rope dangling from your hand. That often is all it takes to remind your partner to keep his lips to himself.

Other biting remedies include pushing your horse's head away from you with your right thumb or with the closed bottom part of your right fist. And, for hard-core biters, a squirt of a mixture of cayenne pepper and lemon juice from a small spray bottle can work wonders. The spray bottle can be tough to manage along with the lead rope, especially for people who are right handed, as you will need to operate the spray mechanism with your left. But a strong, well-aimed spray at a biter's left nostril will go a long way to discourage the activity.

Remember that each of these corrections is a non-event as long as your equine friend is behaving respectfully. Each correction is a classic if/then scenario, and one that horses respond to very well. If he chooses to act inappropriately, then he is automatically corrected. You tell your equine partner, "if you invade my space with your teeth, then your nose will get smacked (or you will breathe pepper spray)." And also, "if you choose to behave, then nothing will happen."

about it. But be persistent, use the zigzag technique, and he will soon be walking alongside you.

WORKING WITHOUT A NET

Now that you and your equine partner can walk, trot, stop, and turn correctly with no behavioral issues, you are ready to try it without a halter or lead. Be sure you are in an enclosed area (a round pen or smaller type of area works better than a larger field or pasture), and remove the halter and lead. Start by positioning yourself exactly as you would if your partner were wearing his usual headgear. Ask your horse to "walk" or "walk on" and begin moving forward. If he does not respond correctly, bring your right arm up under his jawline and give a little tug. If he still does not respond, you may have to transition to this activity by draping a lead rope around his neck before trying again with just your voice and body cues.

Without the halter or lead, you can practice turning, stopping, and changes in gait, while making note of your partner's strengths and weaknesses. Then you can revisit the weaker areas with the halter and lead, before trying again without.

RESULTS!

In a small, enclosed area, you and your equine partner are now walking, trotting, turning, and stopping without benefit of headgear. How cool is that? You are beginning to work very well as a team. Now, you more easily recognize your equine partner's body language and the look in his eye. You feel, rather than see, the tiniest bit of hesitation, and are able to encourage and correct much sooner than you could before you began this activity.

You also have probably noticed your partner's eagerness to please, and our next activity rewards this effort by developing play times and areas for you and your equine friend.

PLAYTIME

One of my youth horses was a tall Appaloosa gelding that I named Ben. His mother was my little mare Snoqualmie, and the two of them could not have been more different. She was short and fat while he was tall and thin. She instantly understood every new thing I introduced to her, while I had to repeat lessons over and over with Ben. Snoqualmie was an escape artist, while Ben enjoyed playing with rocks.

From the time he was very young, Ben found toys to play with. I'd often find him in the pasture with a large rock in his mouth, or sometimes a good-sized branch. He liked to stand with his front feet in the old bathtub we used as a water trough and splash all the water out of it. A special treat was whenever a tractor went by the farm. There was something about the look, sound, and movement of a John Deere that completely captivated him.

Objects also fascinated Ben, and I discovered that if I could find new toys for him to play with, he actually learned faster. Another plus was the fact that his new toys exposed Ben to many odd sounds and sights that prepared him well for a career as a show horse. Years later, when a child's kite unexpectedly landed in the middle of an outdoor show ring during a saddleseat pleasure class, Ben was the only horse that did not spook. And in a trail class, he may sometimes have tripped over the poles, but he was never flustered by a paisley-patterned tent, or a colorful bunch of balloons. To Ben, these were simply new toys to eagerly explore.

Horses who are isolated from the unexpected things in life typically become anxious in unfamiliar situations. Imagine spending your life on a desert island, only to be uprooted and dropped in downtown Manhattan. The experience is similar to a horse who has never been off the farm being taken to a parade, or a first-time trail horse encountering a train. Each situation would be completely overwhelming. This is why it is important to reach into your toolkit to find all the odd and crazy (and safe) objects you can use to stimulate your equine friend's mind. For example, if your partner has been exposed to lots of different types of noises, she will have a point of reference to reassure herself that new noises are not threatening. I recently rode on a trail in a park where a track meet was taking place, and the sound of the starter's gun unnerved some of the horses, even though the track meet was on the other side of the park. The horses were unnerved because they had no safe point of reference for the sound.

Toys provide two kinds of learning experiences for horses. The first is the opportunity to take a break from the more serious side of interactions with humans and find new ways to play. The second is the chance to explore new objects in a protected environment and in the process, discover safety, likes, and dislikes.

In learning to play with toys, your equine partner can develop a more balanced relationship with you. But think how she must feel. Every time your horse sees you, you ask her to do something *you* want to do. Plus, you fully expect her to readily comply. Playtime levels the field in such a way that it does not threaten your position as the boss of the partnership. It also allows your partner to further express her likes and dislikes and for the two of you to forge an even closer bond.

GROUND RULES OF THE GAME

In establishing playtime, designate a different area from where you do your other work with your equine friend. This helps to establish in your friend's mind the rules and boundaries of play, and discourages play attitude during training sessions. The area should be enclosed, and no other horses should be in the enclosure. The size of the area does not matter; however, a stall is probably too small.

Nacho's Ball Game

Nacho has a love-hate relationship with a large red, white, and blue therapy ball that is sometimes used at Saddle Up! to help riders learn balance. Nacho has another use for the ball. He loves to have his human partner roll the ball toward him or past him. He then can choose whether to use his nose to roll the ball back to his partner, kick the ball with a foreleg, or grab it in his teeth and shake it. He rarely tires of the game, but sometimes he becomes frustrated when he can't get the ball going in the manner he wants it to go. Then Nacho can get a little aggressive with the ball. Once he shook it so hard he somehow got it wedged between his legs and he ended up sitting down, staring at the ball in disbelief. When he picked himself up, he purposefully turned his back to the ball, and then stole a few glances backward at it. After a few minutes, Nacho decided the allure of the ball was too much and resumed playing with it.

Watching Nacho play with the ball is an interesting process, because he plays and takes his frustration out on the therapy ball in the same way he plays and takes his frustration out on other horses. When Nacho is playing, he wiggles his behind more than usual. His ears swivel both forward and sideways, and he stares intently at his toy, or the horse he is interacting with. When the play turns frustrating, however, Nacho first swings his head from side to side, then paws or stomps with his left front leg. If those actions do not turn the situation around to his liking, he then sticks his nose out, pins his ears, and finally will bite.

It is important to recognize your equine partner's signs of both play and frustration because, like Nacho, your partner's signs will most likely be the same when dealing with other horses, and with you. If I am introducing a new concept to Nacho and he begins shaking his head, I know I need to quickly move on to an interest he is more comfortable with. A few minutes later, when he is in a more solid frame of mind, I can come back to the new activity. If I ignore Nacho's warning signs, we end up butting heads and have a very unproductive session.

Nacho tries to grab a big ball as it rolls by. This is a game he rarely tires of.

The game rules are simple:

1. While your equine partner may explore, lick, bite, paw, or chew on a toy, she may not do the same with you.

2. You provide the toy, and she plays with it.

Some interactive play can develop, and that is good, but you need to make quite clear with your firm voice, body language, and facial expressions, that she is not to play roughly with you in the same manner she plays with her equine friends.

GAMES

Like Nacho, your partner may develop a fondness for his own version of soccer. Nacho also sometimes will fetch. If you throw a toy about ten feet away from him, he often picks it up and brings it back for you to do all over again. Sometimes he will pick up a small stuffed animal from the top of a barrel, carry it to another barrel, and drop it there.

My colt, Ben, could be encouraged to "sweep" his paddock with a leafy branch, or to go through the pasture and pull carefully placed colorful rags out of a tree, or off a fence. You and your partner will develop your own games and your own form of play by developing interests and exploring the natural curiosity of your horse. Remember that your horse will make up the rules as much as you do, so you have to be alert to what your partner is telling you. Here are a few ideas to get you started:

1. The Dressage Game: Buddy is an intelligent, retired Fourth-level dressage horse and loves upper-level work, although his aging body no longer allows for much of it under saddle. I found that if we do a simple walk-trot dressage pattern from the ground, Buddy remembers it. My game with Buddy is to lead him through the pattern once, then remove the halter and walk or jog next to him as he does the pattern again. He often curls his upper lip at the successful completion of one of these patterns.

2. The Flag Game: If your horse likes to hold things in his mouth, place towels or scraps of cloth in his pasture or around the arena, then lead him up to the item and encourage him to pick it up. He will make up the rules from there, possibly dashing the

cloth against the ground, twirling it in the air, or dropping it on a log. Your part in the game could be to replace the cloth in the same spot, or to direct your horse's attention to another cloth.

3. The Toy Grab: Put several toys in a big box or bucket and allow your partner free rein. The game might involve him dumping the contents out and you putting them back in, or he could choose one and fling it into the air, while you "retrieve."

4. Kickball: Roll a large ball slowly toward your horse. Chances are he will either nudge it with his nose or paw at it and send it rolling back to you. Or, he might grab it in his teeth and throw it in the air. Nacho sometimes will even hold a pom-pom in his mouth and use it to roll the ball toward a goal. You can then roll the ball back to your horse and repeat the game.

PLAYTIME OR WORKTIME

By now you should have discovered the basic signs your equine friend gives when she likes something, and also when she does not. With new toys, there is usually a short period of interest, followed either by play or by disinterest. It may take a few times with a toy to find out whether your horse really does not like that particular toy, or if she just was not interested at a particular time. As a child, you may have loved playing hide-and-seek, but there were probably times that you preferred doing something else, even when the game was offered to you. Your equine partner has similar feelings and may not always be in the mood to play, so be patient and try offering play at different times.

Some horses play better before you ride or do other activities together. They burn off excess energy and are able to make the mental transition to a more serious mode without very much difficulty. Other horses cannot make that transition, so play should be offered after other things are accomplished. You may choose a specific day of the week when you just play with your equine friend. Give it time and you will find the perfect combination for you both.

TOYS, TOYS, AND MORE TOYS

Like a child, your equine friend can make a toy out of just about anything. The important factor is safety. If a potential toy has sharp points,

Nacho can turn anything into a toy, even a plastic bag.

or areas that could easily break if dropped or if a horse bit it more than tentatively, it should not be introduced.

Start your play session with three or four different types of possible toys outside of the play area. At first, the toys should be those that do not make noise or have movement. If you offer, for example, a blue stuffed cat, make sure the cat does not emit a loud "meow" and move its legs when squeezed. Let your equine friend get used to the color, size, and feel of a regular stuffed toy before you add sound and movement to the mix. Bring in each toy one at a time to show to your horse. In addition to stuffed animals, foam rubber balls make good starter toys.

If your equine friend is a little nervous around the new toy, you can put a halter and lead on her and use your whoa cue to help her settle down. Then go back to your desensitization techniques and rub the toy all over her while talking softly in a reassuring voice. As soon as you feel your friend relax, drop the toy on the ground at her side where she can see it (rather than directly in front of her where she can't), or place it on top of a fence post for her to look at. Then stand back and see what happens. If your horse shows interest instead of fear, jump back to the introduction phase and place the toy where she can explore it.

Some horses will look to you for permission. When a new toy is introduced to Lucky, he first explores it with his muzzle, then turns to his human partner for permission to go further. He understands an encouraging nod and tone of voice, and will only go back to the toy once he receives them. Other horses dive right in, and you have to keep an eye out to be sure they are not destroying the toys, or doing anything to injure themselves.

If your equine partner shows no interest, try another similar toy. She may not like the color, shape, or texture of the first one you offered. Or, she just may not be in the mood to play. Make note of the toys your partner has rejected. After several rejections over a few days' or weeks' time, it is safe to say a particular toy holds no interest for your equine friend. And after a while, you will begin to get a feel for what she is—and is not—going to like. With a human friend or family member, you develop a good idea of the things he or she likes, and your horse is no different. Given time, you will be able to provide toys that will stimulate and interest your equine friend for a long time to come.

Many horses prefer toys in a certain category and sometimes in a specific situation. Valentino likes toys that move, while Lucky prefers inanimate toys. Nomo will play when a human partner is present, but not by herself. Lady does not want to play when she is hungry. Nelson enjoys watching toys that move in some sort of rhythm, and Nacho will turn any object into a plaything, given the chance.

TOYS THAT MOVE

Once you have gone through your arsenal of toys that do not move or make sound, you can add movement. Large balls that roll, streamers like those used in dance routines, and slinkies make good starters. Of course, anything that moves makes some sort of sound if you listen closely enough, but start with toys that are generally silent.

Introduce this group of toys just as you did the others. Because horses see colors, shadows, and depth differently than humans do, I put toys that flash light in the movement category. Your equine friend may perceive a flash of light as movement of an object. A ball that glows when it rolls or a hula hoop that lights up are good examples. Just be sure at this stage that the toy only moves and shows light, and does not make any loud noises.

Once your horse has accepted a moving toy, you can begin some interactive play. Try rolling a large ball slowly toward her, being careful not to bump the ball into her legs. That may still be scary for your equine partner at this stage of the game. See if she responds differently if you roll the ball away from her, from right to left in front of her, or from left to right.

Can you tell if she is more apt to play if you engage her with a slinky from the left, or from the right? Does she paw at the slinky or does she try to grab it with her teeth? If you lay it across her back, does she move forward until the slinky falls to the ground, or does she grab it and pull it off? When you find patterns in her play that give clues to

A slinky is a movement toy, and Nacho shows determination as he tries to grab it. When he succeeds he will carry it in his mouth for a while before flinging it across the round pen. That's my cue to "retrieve" the slinky and begin the game all over again.

her thoughts, moods, and feelings, you have taken another step toward true partnership with your equine friend.

A horse may carry a hula hoop in his mouth or intently track a shiny, slow-flying Frisbee. You can also place an object on your horse's back or hang it on a post. Be careful in the early days of play that you do not become so enthusiastic that you inadvertently frighten your equine friend. Slow, gentle play is best until she builds confidence in the process. You will know if your friend is uneasy or concerned. Sometimes turning a horse loose with the toy in a round pen or a familiar stall will encourage exploration.

TOYS THAT MAKE NOISE

Next try toys that only make sound. A stuffed animal that also squeaks, a doll that speaks, or a handheld computer game can hold a horse's interest for some time. Play here may take a different form, as you can't roll a computer game toward your partner. This type of play is more like show and tell. You can manipulate the doll or game to make certain noises, and then talk with your equine partner about the interesting sounds. It's really a conversation with your horse during which your equine partner will likely exhibit some brand new expressions and behaviors for you to study.

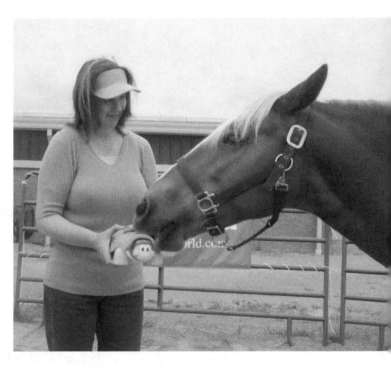

Remember that the idea of play with your equine partner is not just physical, it also includes stretching and engaging your partner's mind. While it is fun to actually play a form of soccer with your horse, it is also interesting to watch as your equine friend recognizes and deciphers the different sounds a doll can make.

Finally, you can begin playing with toys that both move and make sounds. A radio-controlled car that revs it's engine and lights up as it moves, a transformer that makes sounds, a See 'n Say with a lever you can pull to produce certain sounds, and a toy fishing pole with a reel that makes cranking sounds as you pull in your catch all are of interest to the Saddle Up! horses.

Start slowly, or even at a distance, until your equine partner tells you she is ready for closer inspection. Keep an eye on the signals she is giving you, as these will tell you the difference between interest and fear, and acceptance and frustration.

Through playing with toys, I learned that touching a new object with his lips is the way Nacho explores his world.

INTERACTIVE PLAY

By the time you have gone through your arsenal of toys, you should have a good idea of the kinds of toys your equine friend likes and does not like. You may find that there is a category of toy that is a surefire hit, while others hold absolutely no interest.

With your equine friend's favorite toys, you can begin working with her to create interactive play and even develop some games together. This is not something you can go into with any preconceived ideas. Remember, you are in partnership with your horse and she will want input into the game. The concept and rules will most likely be quite simple and will become evident as you go along.

Saddle Up! has a retired Grand Prix warmblood named Samoens who loves to play with an old halter or lead rope. If you hand it to him, he will shake it all around, then fling it into the air. My part of the game is to retrieve it and hand it back to him. If I don't, he becomes impatient and will raise and lower his head frequently to encourage me to get on with the game. We only play in the round pen, and I can signal to him with my verbal and hand whoa signals when it is time for the game to be over. He had a lot of difficulty settling into the demands of working with children with disabilities, and this game helped him through the transition.

RESULTS!

Like many games that children play, engaging your equine partner with toys and games helps her learn in many ways.

1. Play provides a break from routine interaction between you and your equine partner. And even a short break from routine can energize a horse.

2. Play will strengthen the shared experiences and bond between you and your partner.

3. Play will help your friend better understand the more complex areas of her training. When he first began formal groundwork and work under saddle, Nacho had terrible trouble walking and trotting over poles. But by playing with a large ball, Nacho learned to track movement, calculate distances, and maneuver with an object near his feet. He is still not great over poles, but the improvement is like night and day.

4. Play will give your equine partner a stronger foundation in which to reference new shapes and sounds, and develop into a more stable equine companion.

CHAPTER 9

IT'S ALL IN THE VOICE

Years ago, I used to compete in the Egg and Spoon class at local and statewide saddle club shows. The goal was to balance an egg on a spoon while riding at various gaits, and through turns and transitions. The last rider to still have an egg on his or her spoon won the class. My youth horse, Snoqualmie, and I won frequently, not because I was exceptionally skilled in the class, but because she was. While competing in all the other classes at horse shows, Snoqualmie knew to wait for my cue, regardless of what gait or transition the announcer on the loudspeaker called for. But in the Egg and Spoon class, Snoqualmie knew I was busy concentrating on keeping the egg in the spoon, so she took over the responsibility of listening to the announcer, leaving me to deal with the balancing duties.

It got to the point that if Snoqualmie began to trot, I knew that was what the rest of the class was doing. If we reversed, I knew that was the movement the announcer had called for. Snoqualmie was always well balanced, but became especially so on her own during this class. Her smooth gaits became smoother, and her easy transitions were very gentle. We didn't always win, but when we didn't it was invariably due to my poor balancing skills and not her poor listening ability.

Snoqualmie, you see, not only recognized the voice directives of walk, trot, extend, canter, lope, hand gallop, reverse, halt, back, and several others, but she also took great pride in responding correctly to those cues. That was her job, and she loved doing it well.

While not everyone needs a horse that will respond with complete accuracy to an announcer in a horse-show environment, it is helpful for your equine partner to recognize some voice cues. Sometimes sending a voice signal can help you out of a potential safety hazard. A student once told me of getting lost in the woods in the Great Smoky Mountains. When the very narrow path petered out with a huge bobcat sitting on a tree across the trail, there was no room to turn around. Her terrified gelding was frozen in place and didn't acknowledge her rein cues to back. He did, however, respond to her voice cues and cautiously backed thirty feet to a wide spot in the trail where they could maneuver a turn. Fortunately, the bobcat chose not to follow.

I like using voice cues for several reasons. One, it helps to keep my equine partner and me more in tune with each other. One of my first world-caliber horses was a young Appaloosa saddleseat pleasure mare who needed all the help she could get to focus on transitional cues and the requirements of the class. Additionally, when she lost focus, her trot lost cadence. This mare would take a big stride, then a short stride. She'd drift to the left, make a big surge forward, then drift to the right. I learned if I said, "trot, trot" in a singsong voice in time to her stride, that added verbal directive was enough to keep her focused and cadenced both in the show ring and out.

As mentioned in Chapter Four, horses respond to the vowel sound as much as they do to the word itself. And while you can use your own set of voice cues, it is good to keep the vowel sound in mind to help avoid confusion. Horses also respond to the number of syllables in a word. Saddle Up! uses the vocal directive "walk on," and I have noticed that if a volunteer leader says the one-syllable cue of "walk," rather than the two-syllable cue of "walk on," the horses do not respond as well. And while it does not matter what you use, you need to choose one command and stick with it. In a horse's world, consistency is everything.

Tone of voice is also important. In my clinics I ask people to think of a voice directive as a written word. If you ask your equine partner to walk with a question mark at the end of the word, he will think he also has the option to not walk. But, if you ask your friend to walk

Lucky shows his attentiveness to the whoa cue with alert ears and with his body, which is turned toward his human partner.

with either a period or an exclamation mark at the end of the word, he understands that his only choice is to walk.

Remember that voice cues are an additional aid. When mounted, you also cue your partner with your seat, hands, legs, and shifts of weight. On the ground you only have your body position and facial expressions, in addition to your voice, so each of these aids becomes that much more important.

THE BASICS

I like to teach voice cues on the ground during the longeing (pronounced LUN-jing) process. Longeing a horse involves standing in the center of a circle, while your equine friend moves around the perimeter of the circle at different gaits. Longeing can be used to condition horses that for some reason cannot be ridden, to burn off excess energy before riding, and for training purposes. In addition to voice cues, longeing can teach a horse to take a canter departure from a walk, improve other gait transitions, and help with balance and collection, among other things.

Only a few pieces of equipment are needed: a halter, a longe line either with or without a chain at the end, a longe whip, and, if desired,

The Longe Whip

Before you begin, it is important that you know how to use a longe whip. It is very long and can be awkward, so practice without your equine partner. Work with the whip by slowly raising and lowering it using your wrist. Then work it side to side. As you become more comfortable, increase the speed of your wrist action. This will help you gain more control. You can make the whip crack by slowly bringing your wrist up, then quickly snapping it down. This also works in a sideways motion. Slowly turn your wrist to the right, and then snap it to the left. After a little practice, you should gain good control, and a good, sharp crack.

Finally, switch hands. When longeing, you will need to be as adept at using the whip with your left hand as you are with your right. Set up a small target, such as a water bottle on top of a fence. When you can knock the water bottle off to the left, right, and backwards by cracking the whip with each hand, you are ready to begin a longeing session.

gloves. The gloves can increase your grip on the longe line and also prevent rope burns. They are handy to have if your horse pulls on the line or is exceptionally exuberant.

FREE LONGEING

Longeing looks easy, but it can be difficult to do well. A round pen is the ideal place to begin because you can learn to longe without using a longe line. The first thing to remember about longeing is to not get tangled up in the line, as you could be dragged, so if longeing is new to you, it is often easier to learn without having to deal with a long, unwieldy piece of cotton or nylon rope. Free longeing (done without the longe line) also allows a horse new to the longeing process to better balance himself. If you do not have a round pen, you can still teach your equine partner to longe using a longe line in a larger area, and we will get to that in just a minute.

Remember that horses respond to you based on where your body is in relation to theirs. If you are behind a horse's center of gravity he will move forward; if you are in front of it, he will stop or back up. In either case, you are driving the horse in the direction you want him to go by positioning your body.

GETTING STARTED

To begin longeing, position your partner at the edge of a round pen facing right, or clockwise. Imagine that your equine friend's nose is one point of a triangle and his tail another, while your body makes up the third point. You can adjust the angles of the triangle by moving forward or back, depending on where and how fast you want your equine partner to go.

When standing, a horse's center of balance is just behind the withers, so position your body so that your point in the triangle is somewhere behind that area. Hold the longe whip in your left hand, point it toward your horse's tail, and think of the whip as an extension of your arm.

Most horses instinctively sense that when you raise the tip of the whip they are to move forward, and when the tip is down they are to slow or stop. So be conscious of whether your whip is pointing up or down as you may inadvertently be giving your equine friend mixed signals and confusing him. Also know that if you accidentally step in front of his center of balance, he will think you are asking him to stop.

To get your equine friend to move forward, stand in the center of the round pen behind his center, raise the tip of your whip up, say his name, and ask him to walk or walk on. Be sure to speak with a period at the end of your directive, and not a question mark. Chances are, your friend will remember his previous leading training and begin to move forward. If not, repeat his name and the verbal cue, and wave the tip of the whip at him. You can also cluck or kiss to him, or step further behind his center. Remember always to first position yourself and the whip, then use the verbal cues, and lastly, wave or crack the whip.

Valentino canters easily while being free longed. Free longeing keeps pressure off a horse's head and neck, but can teach a human partner about the importance of body position in relation to a horse's center of balance.

If your partner chooses to turn and face you, read the signs he is giving you. Is he licking and chewing with his head lowered? That means he wants to obey but may be confused. Stay relaxed, step toward his right side, and use pleasant (but firm) verbal cues and your right hand to wave his face away from you. As soon as he begins moving, position yourself back in the triangle with your left arm and the whip pointing toward his tail.

Or is he standing with his head raised and his ears back? That means he is saying, "I really don't want to do this!" Use the same actions as for the first type of horse, but much more firmly. Your facial expression and body posture will be all business and your verbal cues will have exclamation points on the end. Instead of waving the whip at him, make it crack. At this point in your relationship, he will back down quickly and get with the program.

Right now all you want is forward movement. If your partner decides to go overboard by trotting, galloping, or bucking around the pen, let him. It is a losing proposition to ask any horse for a transition when he or she is in the middle of a bucking spree. Wait until he begins to tire, then drive him forward with your voice, body, and whip for another circuit or two around the pen. Only when you believe he is listening to you and ready to quit should you ask for his attention.

Once he has settled down and you have consistent forward movement at the walk, you can ask for a stop. Just step forward (ahead of your equine friend's center), hold out your right hand in the halt sign, drop the tip of your whip to the ground, and say whoa. Most horses will stop and turn to face you. Some who have show-ring or other higher-level training will stop exactly where they are, still facing right. Either way, once your friend has halted, tell him "good boy" from your spot in the center of the pen. Then step back behind his center and ask him to walk. Repeat the walk/whoa transition in both directions until you and your partner are comfortable with it.

Your equine friend should also move away from you if you ask. For example, if your partner turns toward you and walks a few steps before stopping, you can shoo him away with your hands. At the same time as you make shooing movements, take a step toward him, call your horse's name and then ask him to walk or turn. Responding to a series of cues to move away is also a safety net, just in case your partner invades your space.

REVERSE DIRECTION

When reversing, you may eventually get your partner to change direction simply by making a circular motion with your hand along with the vocal directive of "change" or "turn." But for now you will probably have to walk up to your horse and physically turn him around. It is important to always turn your partner toward the center of the circle. Later on, if he is in the middle of a playful buck and flips directions, he will be in the habit of turning his head toward you, rather than his heels. After you have him in position, be sure to use your verbal and hand signal for whoa, so that he does not follow you back to the center of the round pen. Going the opposite direction, you will also need to switch hands, as the whip should always be carried in the hand that is closest to the horse's tail.

Be sure to keep an eye on the physical signs your equine friend is giving, as you do not want him to become bored. If your partner is learning faster than you are, break the session into several short ones or spread them out over several days. You want to be sure boredom does not set in for your horse and the breaks will help keep his interest level high.

TROT

When your equine friend is circling well at the walk in both directions and is performing the walk/whoa and whoa/walk transition on cue (and when you feel comfortable), ask for the trot. Remember the sequence of first stepping back behind his center of balance, keeping the tip of the longe whip pointed up, and saying your partner's name. Saying his name before any other verbal cue gets his attention and pulls him away from his daydreams of being surrounded by lovely mounds of alfalfa. Only then, when you are in position and have your horse's attention, should you ask for the gait.

You can practice moving your equine partner from a slow trot to a faster one by repositioning your body further back and by raising the end of the whip. Watch your friend during the process to refine your cues and to determine exactly how much (or little) of each cue you need. Each horse is different, but before too long you will both be in sync and will be working well together. Eventually, you can add in a voice cue of "extend" or "more" to ask for an extension of any gait. I have heard people use the word "faster" but it sounds too much like "canter" to me, so I use the other words.

CANTER

When you are both doing well with forward movement at the trot, and with the necessary gait transitions, you are ready to canter. Even if you prefer Western riding to English, I prefer the word "canter" instead of the word "lope." Lope has a long "o," which duplicates the vowel sound in "whoa." Additionally, they are both one-syllable words. As horses often listen to the vowel sound and the number of syllables, rather than the specific word itself, "canter" is easier for a horse to distinguish.

If your horse is well trained, you can ask for the canter from a walk. Otherwise, ask for it from the trot. Remember, when longeing you only want to ask your friend to do something you feel he has a good shot at doing. At the trot it is easy to position your body farther behind your partner's center, raise the whip higher, call your horse's name and then say "canter." Unless a horse is well trained, if you ask from the walk he will trot for a while anyway, so to avoid your partner thinking that the word canter also means trot, you may as well ask from the trot. As time goes on, and as you and your equine partner become more fine-tuned in longeing technique, you can ask for the canter from an increasingly slower trot. When he is taking it well from a jog, and when you can ask after only a few jogging steps, then you can try a walk/canter transition.

When you are first getting used to the canter, do not worry too much about leads. Early on it is enough that your friend is cantering. But as you and he become more familiar with the cues, you can bring him back to a walk or trot and ask for a new transition whenever he picks up the wrong lead. Be sure to praise your partner whenever he correctly responds to a cue. We all like to be recognized for doing good work!

The reason it is important that your horse be on the correct lead at the canter is for balance. If he is on the wrong lead he will have trouble balancing correctly. To determine if your equine friend is on the correct lead, watch his legs as they move. If you are going clockwise, your friend should first move his left hind, then his right hind and left front together, and finally his right front. The right front leg will reach further forward than the left one will. Going counterclockwise the pattern will be reversed: right hind, left hind and right front together, and finally left front.

USING THE LONGE LINE

When you and your horse have mastered longeing without a longe line in a round pen, it is time to add the line and work in a larger area. If you do not have use of a round pen you will start here, but you still should be familiar with the concepts of free longeing, and in use of the longe whip, as the steps you initially take with the longe line will be identical.

Here are a few safety considerations for longeing with a longe line.

1. Always longe in an enclosed area such as a riding ring, arena, or paddock. If your equine friend gets away from you, then he will remain safe.

2. If your partner pulls hard enough to knock you off balance, let go. Nothing is worth being dragged, and you are, after all, in an enclosed area.

3. Hold the longe line with the first point of contact being the heel of your hand, rather than between your thumb and forefinger. This will give you extra grip and leverage and help prevent rope burns if the line is pulled through your hand.

4. If you have gloves and it is not so hot that your hands sweat inside them, use them. Gloves add to your grip and can prevent rope burns.

5. Keep your elbow tucked into your side. If your elbow is out away from your body, your shoulder is likely to get yanked.

6. Hold the loose end of the longe line either looped in your free hand in a figure eight (as you would hold the loose end of a lead rope) or let the end run through your whip hand and dangle where you will not step on it or get tangled up in it. Holding the end in a figure eight is best, but some people have so much trouble coordinating their two hands, the whip, and the play of the line that it is a lower safety risk to leave the line dangling on the ground. Regardless, always keep two hands on the line.

Begin by attaching the longe line to the ring under the halter. Only if your horse bucks, plays, and pulls should you run a chain through

Longeing in a larger area with a longe line, Valentino responds to a cue to trot as soon as I raise the tip of the longe whip.

the ring on the side closest to you, under the chin, and clip it to the ring by the jaw on the opposite side. When you switch directions, you will need to reverse the chain manually. Then step to your partner's side and begin playing out the line as you encourage forward motion. Once you and your partner master longeing (or any other activity) a chain should not be needed.

The big difference for you between free longeing and using a longe line is that you will feel some pull on the line. You can also vary the size of the circle. With free longeing in a round pen, the circle is limited to the size of the enclosure. On a longe line, if your equine friend gets too carried away or if you are having trouble controlling him, you can always reel him in to create a smaller circle. And the process of making smaller and larger circles is actually good for your horse's balance and helps to stretch different groups of muscles.

PROBLEM SOLVING

If you and your partner are both experienced longers, you will not have too many problems. But a few difficulties may develop if either one of you is new to the process. Here are some tips that will help you stay on the right path:

1. If your horse initially wants to buck and play, let him. He is just like a second grader at recess. He will not listen to you until he has burned off a little excess energy. Don't encourage him, as he may become overly rambunctious and hurt himself, but do not discourage him. Neutrality is the best course of action here. It might also be helpful to drop the whip until he settles down.

2. Only ask your friend for a gait change when you feel he is ready to give you the correct response. You will know when his head drops and his ears begin to swivel toward you that the time is right. If your horse is ready to quit, be sure you give a walk or whoa cue before he does it on his own. It is very important that your partner understand that you are the only one who calls the shots.

3. If your partner has more difficulty going one direction than the other, go back to leading him from that side. When he performs well with you at his side, gradually move away from him as you lead. Sometimes you have to be more conscious of your body position on a specific side. It helps to be well behind his center so you can drive him forward.

4. Do not tolerate flipping directions. If you ask your horse to track right, he should track right. Suddenly switching directions can be a safety issue. If it happens, ask for an immediate halt and firmly turn him in the original direction. Be aware that it might happen again, so be ready to drive your friend forward before he turns.

RESULTS!

Voice cues and longeing require both partners to be intently focused on each other. With that focus comes a closer understanding of how the other thinks, works, and plays. Being well versed in both skills is critical to the following activities, so be sure you are completely comfortable with the process and that your partner is responding well.

MAKE SOME NOISE

10

A few months ago, I was leading one of the Saddle Up! miniature horses through a crowd at a horse event when a girl of about ten spotted us from fifty feet away. The girl, who was wearing a bright pink dress, threw her arms up over her head and shrieked, "Looook!!" as she ran toward us. It was enough to scare me half to death, not to mention the rest of the crowd and the mini. Fortunately, someone at a nearby picnic table grabbed the little girl before she could fling herself upon us. The mini, bug-eyed by this time, jumped forward and spun around to get a better look at her very vocal new admirer, but settled quickly when I said, "whoa."

In thinking back over the situation, even though the sight of a bright pink blur headed straight for us was unnerving, what was actually scary was the earsplitting, high-pitched shriek. The sound was also what first grabbed my attention, and the attention of the crowd around us.

As you know by now, the three main areas of desensitization are audio (sound), visual (sight), and movement (which involves tracking and perception). Horses have much better hearing than we humans do, but they also hear differently. A horse's ear moves almost 180 degrees, so it can pick up sound from various directions. Given

A plastic ball bouncing gently in a little tin pot can make a huge racket.

two ears, that means a horse can zone in on a specific sound in an almost 360-degree circle.

Horses also hear higher frequencies than humans do, and can pick up lower frequencies through vibration in the ground. Have you ever heard the old adage about watching a herd of horses to predict the weather? It's true. Horses can feel the rumbling vibration of thunder and hear a wind coming from several miles away, long before a human can sense any kind of a change. Remember that in the wild, horses are prey animals and their very lives depend, in part, on having an excellent sense of hearing.

Because horses pick up on frequencies we cannot hear, because they can hear sounds made even miles away, and because horses evaluate every sound that comes into their ears as a potential death threat, it is important to take extra time in desensitizing horses to various sounds in different environments.

Just because your equine partner is comfortable with you shaking bells around her body in the comfort of her stall, it does not necessarily translate that she will be comfortable with this in the cross-tie area, in her pasture, in your riding ring, or in any place other than her stall. Remember that horses pigeonhole items, to the extent that a large brass bell is a completely different object than a group of small silver bells. And to a horse, a fan blowing outside her stall can be different than an identical fan blowing in the arena.

While some will be new, you and your equine partner will already have worked with many objects that produce sound. The difference here is that you will be combining one or more sounds with another activity, such as leading. Another difference is that in the process, you will be leaving the safety of your regular training area.

If you listen closely, you can actually hear the difference between the sound of a whistle blown outdoors, and the same whistle blown inside the aisle of a barn. Interior walls, flooring, and roofs can cause echoing, muffling, and amplification that are not found outside, and each of these elements can alter the pitch, volume, and intensity of the noise. And, a horse's sensitive hearing will pick up even more differences than will a human ear.

SOUND IDEAS

Stepping outside your horse's "safe" area is a big move in trust and confidence for both of you. But if you have done your homework, the following activities should be relatively easy. Remember to go slowly, and only provide as much sound as your partner is comfortable with. You never want to frighten your friend, only to interest her. She will tell you when she is ready to step it up.

PLAY A CD

If you haven't yet tried one of the CDs that are made specifically for desensitizing horses, now is the perfect time. If you do not have access to this type of CD, try playing different genres of music on the radio, or even a book on tape. You might even find one of the old radio shows on cassette or DVD, complete with sound effects and dramatic music.

It is easy to put your horse in her stall, put a CD in the player, and go about your other chores. Be sure to keep an eye on her though, as you will want to take note of the sounds that interest her or those that make her uneasy. You can do this by watching the physical reactions she is having to the different sounds. She will tell you if the noises make her irritated, interested, or angry, or if she wants to ignore them. Then see if your equine friend has a different reaction if you turn the volume up or down, or if you move the CD player closer or farther away.

HUMAN SOUNDS

Ask any ten-year-old boy who knows how to make an armpit fart, and he will tell you that we humans can make a lot of unique sounds, and not all the sounds come from our mouths. One activity that involves a nonverbal human sound is to lead your equine friend in a familiar area while raising your arm and dropping it on your thigh. Depending on how hard and fast your hand hits your thigh, it can make quite a loud clapping noise. Remember, though, that any kind of overhand

Observing Reactions

Nelson and Lady usually sleep through one of these CD sessions, and Nacho used to show interest, but now he nods off as well. Nomo splays her feet apart and blows air through her nose for a while before settling down. Valentino sticks his head out his stall door and bangs on the door with a front hoof as soon as the sounds come on. Lucky retreats to the farthest corner of his stall.

What, exactly, does this tell me? One, Nelson, Lady, and Nacho probably will not startle at sudden noises. And they usually don't. Two, Nomo, despite being an older horse, is always going to be wary of something new. And new to her means new to her that day. Nomo spent many years being a Thoroughbred broodmare, so her survival instincts may be stronger than those of Lady, who is a pony, or those of a gelding. Nomo is used to being the "watcher," the lead mare who alerts the herd of impending danger. In a herd environment a mare of this status has more responsibility than other horses, and this translates to her interaction with humans. And, as a Thoroughbred, she is naturally higher strung than a Haflinger, or most Quarter Horses. Three, Valentino is brave

and curious. It may be youthful indiscretion, but he likes to be right in the middle of the action and would really like to take a closer look at the CD player. And four, Lucky is a little insecure. He wants either his human or his herd to be there to tell him what to do. In the absence of either, he will freeze and do nothing.

This information is critical to moving forward with your individual equine friend. I have to approach Nacho and Lucky on completely different terms. If I am not bold with Nacho, he will not respect me; however, boldness intimidates Lucky. With Lucky, I need to be confident, but not bold. This translates to my body posture and facial expressions when I present new things to each horse, and how I specifically engineer the presentation. With Nacho, I have to remain fairly close by to ensure that he does not get carried away and play with a new toy so aggressively that he destroys it. With Lucky, it is better to leave a new object in his stall or feed bin for a few days so he can think about it. There is zero chance that Lucky will break something by being too hard with it. Mentally, Lucky needs to be encouraged, and Nacho needs to be restrained.

movement can seem threatening to a horse, so it is best to start this activity with slow and quiet movements.

This is one of the few times I will ever lead a horse with the lead rope in just one hand, as I need the other arm to be free so I can raise and lower it. Because you are leading with just one hand, be sure you are in some kind of enclosed area. If your friend pulls away, she will still be safe in the enclosure.

Also be sure to lead with the hand that is closest to the halter and raise and lower the arm that is farthest away from the horse. You can talk to your equine friend as you lead and clap, increasing the speed and sound of the claps as she becomes more familiar with the sound and movement. Of course, what you do on the left side of your partner, you will also do on the right side, so once she has accepted the activity on the left you can switch hands and sides and move to the right.

Also, if you are a person who has trouble walking and chewing gum, you might practice walking while doing the arm clap by yourself, before you try it with your partner.

Nomo shows a lot of interest in normal human sounds, such as clapping.

Another nonvocal noise humans can make is stomping. Horses can become wary when a human stomps because stomping is often accompanied by angry behavior. So start with little stomps. As it becomes clear to your friend that the soft stomping is only noise (and does not include anger), you can increase the tempo and the force of the impact to create a louder noise. Also try stomping on different surfaces. It is hard to create much noise on gravel. But other surfaces, such as wood, make a wonderfully loud sound. When your equine partner tells you he is fine with the arm clap and the stomping individually, try stomping and clapping at the same time.

Nomo uses her ears and body to tell her human partner that she is uneasy with the unusual arm movement and thigh slap. Walking over the bridge adds an additional element that Nomo has to think about.

Two-handed clapping and slapping the top or side of your riding helmet also make different nonverbal sounds.

SHRIEK, YELL, AND SHOUT

Of course, humans do make lots of vocal sounds as well. Try a loud shout or yell, or even a series of them, as you lead your friend around a familiar place. Regularly change the pitch, volume, and tempo of your sounds, and if one elicits a stronger reaction than the others, back the volume and frequency down a little, but stay with it until your friend relaxes. Horses always look to the dominant partner of their group for confirmation and support. So even though it is you who is making all the noise, if your body posture and facial ex-

pression indicate all is well, your equine partner should soon relax. All you are doing is making unique noises routine.

Then try an arm clap and a shout together while leading your horse around the arena, or through a pasture. Or, gather a group of friends together who will clap, stomp, shout, and yell as you lead past them. Remember, though, that your equine friend's hearing is better than yours. So take care that no shouts go directly into your horse's ear.

PLAY THE RADIO

If your voice tires, try carrying a portable radio, Walkman, iPod, or MP3 player with you while you groom your partner, or while you walk her out to the pasture. Switch between big band music, talk, jazz, and pop to see what soothes your friend and what makes her excited. You did this activity before, but in the safety of a stall, grooming area, or round pen. Now you are moving into new areas such as a pasture or riding ring that may not feel as safe to your friend. Because of this, you may get results that differ from what you noticed before.

SING ALONG

Unless you have a voice that is as out of tune as mine, sing along with your favorite songs as you practice leading and arm claps. When I was a teenager I knew a local trainer who routinely sang to his horses to relax them. Whenever he introduced a new concept or encountered something unexpected, he broke into song and his horses immediately calmed down. Sometimes he accompanied himself by slapping his thigh or snapping his fingers in time to his song. The steady rhythm did its magic and helped his horses focus on the new situation or skill.

I often competed against this trainer in Western pleasure classes, and he had a young stallion that especially did not like the fifties-era country twang that one horse show played over its loudspeakers during classes. To distract his horse, during competition the trainer rode around the ring softly and slowly singing "Three Blind Mice" as he snapped his fingers in time to his song. As soon as the singing began, his youngster quickly calmed down and ably won the class.

WHISTLE WHILE YOU WORK

If you do not ordinarily whistle, the sound can provoke interesting reactions from your equine friend. Once he is accustomed to the sound, combine it with grooming, or stomping while leading. Many people whistle to a farm dog across a field, or to a friend while working with a horse, so it is important to introduce your partner to both the piercing and the melodic kinds of whistling.

BRING ON THE BELLS

From deep, booming church bells to the clank of a cowbell to the tinkly sound of a bell on a cat's collar, each bell sounds unique. Try leading your horse while carrying and ringing a variety of bells. The bells will sound different when you walk than when you jog, so try both, and from both sides of your partner. You can ring them in unusual rhythm patterns, ring them softly, and ring them loudly, but never ring them in a way that is more than your equine friend can handle.

Once I took a horse to a competition at an outdoor facility that was yards away from a large country church. The sound of the church bells booming hourly in the bell tower set almost every horse on edge. It's likely that the noise was so loud it was uncomfortable for the horses to listen to. There is also the vibration factor to consider, and, of course, the novelty. When I knew I would be returning to that particular show grounds, I made a special point to lead my horses in from the pasture while I carried and rang the deepest-sounding bell I could find. After a few weeks of that, the horses ignored the sound and we did much better at the next show.

SHAKE, RATTLE, AND ROLL

Rattles are especially scary to a horse, as rattlesnakes are a natural predator. Also falling into this category are hula hoops with beads inside them, mariachis, and "rain" tubes, which all sound quite similar. Many horses need a little more time with these items as their unease is instinctive, so be patient. When she is ready, you can, for example, combine a rain tube with whistling as you lead your friend into her stall.

OTHER NOISES

Aluminum cans in a plastic bag, or a pie plate and a plastic ball in a paper bag, are both very noisy and provide interesting movement. An old drum can make a nice repetitive sound if you can find someone who has a little rhythm to play it. And a New Year's Eve party favor, a plastic flute, or a toy bugle can all provide interesting experiences for your friend to think over.

RESULTS!

So what, other than making you look very foolish with all the clapping, stomping, and singing, does all of this accomplish? Certainly your equine partner will never come across a person on the trail or on the show grounds who is clapping while holding a bell and a rain tube as he stomps and sings. (Well, maybe if there is a New Age band on site.) But these activities do solidify the trust between you and your partner, and they build confidence in you both. If your horse reacts calmly to these kinds of noises, then there is a good chance she will remain calm when she hears a police siren, or the squeak of a loose piece of aluminum siding as the wind blows through the barn. In that way, the activities further desensitize your equine friend to unusual and unexpected sounds. The activities also give her a safe and solid reference point in which to categorize new sounds that she may later hear.

You also have a stronger reference base for your partner's likes and dislikes. Was she intrigued or nervous when you stomped on wood? Was it difficult for her to get used to your arm movement when doing a thigh slap, or did she accept it right away? How about unusual noises such as musical instruments? Was there one she seemed more interested in, or did she let you know with her body language that she really did not like the noise from a toy trumpet? Your horse's reactions to each noise and each situation will give you further understanding of her thoughts and preferences, which you can use for further understanding.

Finally, combining sounds gives your friend more than one area on which to focus. Having to decipher, categorize, and react to two strange sounds simultaneously causes her brain to multitask and will help her process more advanced directives later on. As you and your equine partner progress through My Horse, My Partner, and through life, there will be more and more situations that require the combining of senses, talents, and experiences, especially in the next chapter.

LET'S DANCE

❦

Sometimes it is best to not know what you are doing. When I was ten or eleven, I competed in a local "bicycle rodeo." We had to weave between closely spaced cones, get mail out of a mailbox, and ride in a tight circle to demonstrate how well we could control our bicycles.

When I got Dondi, my pony, I had no idea what I was supposed to do to fine-tune his leading skills, so I set up an obstacle course similar to that in the bicycle rodeo. We did not have any cones or a portable mail-box, so Dondi and I made circles around a wheelbarrow, pulled pieces of cardboard from cracks in trees, and weaved around sticks I found in the nearby woods and pounded into the ground.

If, like me, you do not have access to more traditional equipment, improvise. Buckets can be used as cones, as can plastic bags partially filled with sand or dirt and tied at the top. Just ensure that whatever you use does not have any jagged edges or splinters, and that it will not poke your equine partner or cause him to slip or trip in any way.

AROUND AND AROUND

By now you realize that horses learn by repetition. Repeat an activity, such as leading, the wrong way, and you have to repeat it correctly twice as often to change the behavior. Lucky likes to hang behind his leader and has probably done that for most of his thirteen or so years. He can lead correctly, but it takes great effort and constant reminders

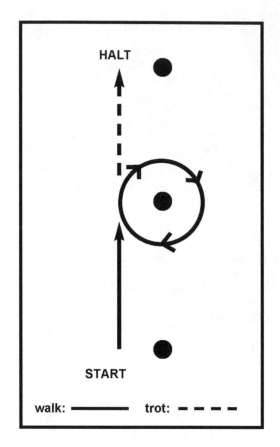

to him to keep up. By being led only in a correct manner, eventually Lucky will forget how to lead improperly and will unconsciously position himself next to his leader, rather than behind. He is already showing significant improvement, but it may take weeks (or months) longer. But at some point he will get it, and repetition is the key.

You have already given your equine friend a good foundation in leading, but now you both are ready for more advanced leading activities: patterns. Set up a pattern by putting several markers in an enclosed area. The markers can be cones, barrels, plastic sand bags, or even pieces of colored paper taped to fence posts. The only important things for your pattern to have are a clear beginning point, a transition marker, and an end point.

For example, if you set up three cones near the center of a paddock, you might lead your friend to the first cone and stop. This is your starting point. Ask your partner to walk in a straight line to the second cone and make a circle around it to the right. Then trot from the second cone to the third and stop.

This sounds very easy, but when you think of all the elements that have to occur for you and your partner to lead this pattern correctly, suddenly it becomes far more difficult.

1. You and your partner have to start together. This is best accomplished by practicing the whoa/walk transition with your equine friend so that he responds instantly and smoothly to your walk cue.

2. You next need to lead a straight line. To do this, fix your eyes on a point in the distance and never waver your gaze. If you look to the left, for example, you will begin to drift to the left, and your horse, of course, will follow you.

3. To make a circle to the right, your friend needs to smoothly move away from you as soon as he senses you moving into his space, or as soon as he feels pressure on his halter. This you

should have accomplished in earlier leading activities. If not, take time to go back and review. The circle also has to be round, and this can take some practice. Think of the circle as four big pieces of pie that make up a whole. If you lead, for example, four steps to create the first piece of the pie, then you should lead an additional four steps to create the next quarter of the pie. Your full circle will contain sixteen steps: four steps, times four pieces of pie. Walking a round circle is another skill that can first be practiced without your equine partner.

Even leading a simple pattern through a series of cones can be difficult to do well. Nelson's lowered head and swiveling ears indicate he wants to do his best.

4. The transition to the trot should take place at the exact point where you began your circle (next to the second cone), and your partner should easily stay alongside you as you pick up the pace.

5. Remember to trot straight by fixing your eyes on a distant point, just as you did at the walk.

6. The transition from the trot to the halt should be immediate, with no walking steps in between, and should occur with your horse's barrel at the last cone. This takes thought, practice, and teamwork.

The described pattern is just one of thousands you can devise for yourself and your partner. A more advanced pattern might be to set

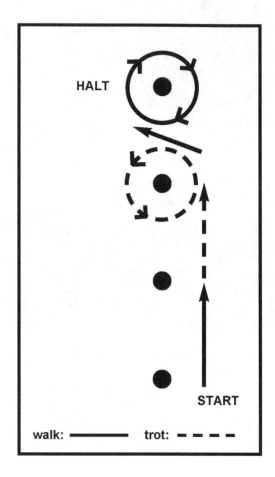

HALT

START

walk: ———   trot: – – – –

up four markers. In this exercise, you and your partner will stand squarely at the first marker, walk a straight line from the first to the second marker, trot from the second to the third marker, then trot a full circle to the left around the third marker, walk from the third to the fourth marker, and walk a full circle to the right around marker four before halting.

The more precise your course is the better, because it forces you and your partner to work as a team. In that teamwork, you become more strongly aware of your partner's little nuances. A twitch of a lip can mean your horse is listening intently, a blink of an eye can mean uncertainty, and a flick of an ear might mean he is bored. But you will never know these things about your equine friend until you work with him on this level, so pay close attention to what your partner is telling you.

As you have seen, a pattern does not have to be complicated for you and your partner to develop as a team, so keep your goals in this area simple at first. Depending on your shared skills, a mutual beginning, straight line, and a stop at a particular point can be a challenge to do well.

As you practice over and over, you might notice your horse automatically stopping at a specific marker, or beginning to turn a circle before you are ready. He needs to learn to wait for you. In real life, you do not want him to stop or transition to a trot every time he sees an orange cone, so it is important to vary the pattern frequently.

Freshening the pattern keeps both you and your partner on your toes. You can still work on simple and specific skills that are harder for you, but in a way that makes both of you think. Do the pattern in reverse by starting at the far end. Put the circle in the middle or turn right instead of left. You can even use new markers, change the location of your work area from an outdoor ring to a paddock, or try imaginary markers such as the third post from the corner, or five steps past the gate.

ADVANCED TURNING

Once you and your equine friend have mastered starting and stopping together, straight lines, and round circles, you can practice more complicated turns. Figure eights and serpentines are both excellent moves because they require smooth changes of direction and balance. It can be tough enough to make one perfect circle, but with a figure eight, you need to make two, and serpentines require a series of perfect loops.

Weaving through a series of tightly spaced markers is a good activity to practice before doing serpentines. You can weave close in, right next to the marker, or loop your partner at a distance that is further away from each one. Experiment to see how tightly you can space the markers in a row before you and your partner have difficulty turning. Depending on the size and build of your equine friend, the markers might be spaced five strides apart, or maybe three. If your weaving takes on the shape of a serpentine, then your markers can be closer together, as you will be making your loop farther away from the marker and the extra distance makes the turn easier. Note that you will probably have to space the markers farther apart for trotting activities that are close to the markers, unless your partner's trot is the stock-horse shuffle.

Before you begin a pattern, decide in your mind what exactly you want to accomplish. Do you want to perform small tight serpentines, or a large figure eight? Instead of round circles, maybe you want to walk squares or egg-shaped figure eights. Will you be walking or trotting your pattern? Are you weaving through four markers or ten? Where and when will you stop?

You can also explore the differences in a turn around a tall vertical pole versus a turn around a shorter marker. The width of your equine partner's barrel can overhang a low or ground marker when you are leading close to it, but leading through tall vertical poles does not allow that comfort. Your horse will really need to bend to get through tall, tightly spaced vertical markers.

UP AND OVER

Walking and trotting over flat poles, raised cavalletti, bridges, plywood, plastic, tarps, and logs is wonderful exercise for your partner, as each requires higher than normal movement of his or her legs. This activity es-

Gates

Try not to plan your stops directly in front of a gate. It is very easy for a bored, tired, or lazy horse to think, "Hmmm . . . I came in the gate; maybe if I go out the gate I can go back to my stall and eat." Then he will think about stopping every time he passes a gate. And if he is thinking about stopping, then he is not paying attention to you. He is not being a team player. There are plenty of other places to stop, so make it a point to keep moving past the exits.

Walking up or over an object is an excellent exercise in trust, and it is also good for your partner's back and hindquarter muscles.

pecially works shoulder and back muscles. Each element also makes an interesting addition to your leading activities. These obstacles can be used in any pattern, figure eight, or weaving exercise. As you progress into more advanced activities, your equine partner's talents and shortcomings will become more evident. In two and a half years of leading and longeing exercises, Nacho has yet to get through a series of flat cavalletti without tripping. This is obviously a difficult activity for him. On the other hand, Valentino rarely ticks a series of raised poles. Nomo always needs to stop to thoroughly inspect a tarp or piece of plastic before very gingerly tiptoeing over it, while Lady never hesitates to plow right on through, no matter what it is.

By now you know many of your equine friend's likes and dislikes, peculiarities and quirks, so you will need to take them, and your partner's individual talents, into consideration in setting expectations for advanced work. While it is a nice eventual goal, today I cannot expect that Nacho will be able to walk over a set of cavalletti without tripping. I can, however, expect that he will try. And he does. Nelson is very laid back, so I cannot expect him to show the same amount of interest or enthusiasm that Lucky does in an activity, but I can expect that Nelson will perform whatever I ask to the best of his ability. And Nelson is very agreeable; he's just not going to get all excited about it.

In adding walk-over obstacles to your leading activities, your goal is the same: to work together as a team with your horse. Never forget that you are partners. If your equine friend needs a little more time at first to investigate a new object, give him that time, then encourage him when he is ready to negotiate it. Also ensure that if you are asking your partner to step on an object, rather than over it, there is no chance of slippage. Tarps or plastic might need to be weighted at the corners, and wood surfaces may need to be roughened. All surfaces should be absolutely dry.

Remember that horses see contrasts more sharply than humans do, so if you are asking your partner to step on a tarp or a piece of plastic, it

may seem to him that you are asking him to step into a bottomless pit. Any time your horse refuses an activity or obstacle, revise your plan and go back to the familiar introduction activities. You may not get your friend to walk across a piece of plywood today, but if you are patient, maybe you will tomorrow.

Remember that a horse cannot see directly behind, so it is important that you face the rear if you are backing.

BACK IT UP

Backing is a great activity because it uses muscles that help develop the horse's power pack, the hindquarters. It is also a leap of faith because a horse cannot see directly behind himself. Your horse has to trust that you will direct him safely around any obstacle, and a successful backing session will build your partner's confidence and trust in you.

Some horses, however, have never been taught to back and will actively resist. Resistance might also occur because he has a sore back, or it might be stubbornness, fear, or even an association with a bad experience. In such situations it is more important than ever that your friend be asked to back correctly. First, turn to face your horse's tail. When leading a horse, you always want to be facing the direction you want to go. Then pull back slightly on the halter and say "back." As soon as your horse takes a step backward, release the pressure on the halter. This is his reward for responding correctly. Repeat the process until you and your partner have taken all the steps you desire.

If your partner actively resists, you may have to settle for one step at a time, followed by effusive praise. When Nacho first came to Saddle Up! he was a driving horse and had been taught *not* to back. It took many months of patiently repeating the process for him to understand that here—without being hooked to a big cart—backing was okay.

What is not okay is to try to push your horse backward. It does not matter how big and strong you are; your equine friend is bigger and stronger. You have to get your horse to the point that he chooses to respond correctly. You can do this with horses who actively resist by tapping the front of your partner's lower leg with a dressage whip as you cue him to back. Remember that the whip is an extension of your arm, and the force you use will be consistent with that of a firm tap of your hand. When you tap, your partner will lift that leg, and when the leg is in the air, you can increase pressure on the halter to shift your partner's weight to the rear. When your partner's leg lands on the ground, it will be half a step behind where it was earlier. Lavish praise every time you do this will have your friend backing smoothly before too long.

Backing a horse is similar to backing a bumper-mounted horse trailer. If you want to move your partner's hindquarters to the right, for example, you need to turn his head to the left. You and your partner can practice zigzagging backward, backing between poles or other markers, and backing figure eights. Or, you can incorporate backing into one of your patterns by requiring your horse, for example, to back four steps after stopping at the third cone. Always position your body in the direction you want to go, and eventually your rear-facing body position itself will serve as another cue to your partner.

TURNS ON THE HINDQUARTERS

A turn on the hindquarters is a turn where the inside back leg does not leave the ground—the front end of the horse essentially "walks" around the hindquarters. This turn is easier to do to the right, as you can walk "into" your partner, encouraging him to shift weight to his hindquarters as he moves away from you, but it can also be done to the left. A good turn on the hindquarters demonstrates the precision with which you and your partner can lead together.

If you are just learning this move, it is helpful to have a friend on hand (or a large mirror) to tell you if you are executing it properly. Begin by facing the direction you want to go, which in this case would be to the right. You should now be facing just ahead of your horse's eye. And your partner should be in tune enough with you to know just by your body position which direction you will ask him to go. Put a little pressure on the halter, both back and to the right, then cluck or kiss as you walk

toward his face. Just ask for a 90-degree turn and stop. If no one is available to help you, check the hoofprints your horse made during the turn to see if he lifted his inside hind—or in this case, right—leg. If he did, you may need to turn into him more, or to put more pressure on the halter.

Another option is to stand with your partner's nose inches away from the sharp corner of a fence. If you turn into him as discussed, he almost has to do a turn on the hindquarters to get out of the corner. A third technique is to first ask for half a step backward, and if you can get it with the left front leg, you are in a perfect position to then turn, face your partner, and ask for a turn on the hindquarters. The half step backward helps your friend shift his weight to the rear, and the left front underneath his body becomes the weight bearing leg, making it easy for the right front to lift up and move sideways to the right.

Take the turn one step at a time until you can easily do 90 degrees. Then begin practicing 180-degree turns (or reverses). A 270-degree, or three-quarter, turn comes next, and before you know it you will be executing perfect 360-degree turns on the hindquarters. Like backing, this turn is excellent exercise because it works lateral, or sideways, groups of muscles that help keep your horse strong. To walk his front

While Lucky is attempting a turn on the hindquarters, it is difficult because his hind legs are not spaced evenly, side by side. Pressure from the halter and the handler's position at Lucky's head encourages him to shift his weight back and to the right, allowing his front legs the freedom to move sideways to the right. When learning this turn, it is helpful to have a spotter or watch where the horse is placing his legs. Later you will be able to tell by the "feel" of the horse if his legs are placed and moving correctly.

When switching sides, be sure to switch hands so the hand directing the horse is always the one closest to him. Now that Lucky's hind legs are properly positioned, he can more easily shift his weight from right to left and move his body around his hindquarters.

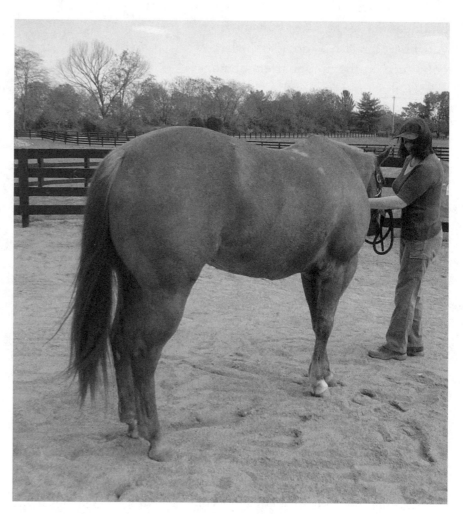

end around his back end, your partner has to take sideways steps, crossing his front feet in the process. These turns can also be incorporated into your patterns.

Once you can make this turn to the right, you can practice to the left. This is more difficult for several reasons. Turning right, or into your horse, is a reminder that you are the dominant partner in the relationship. In turning to the left, you are pulling your partner toward you, which is always awkward. You also have to turn your body away from your partner when going to the left, which can be a safety issue. You and your friend are briefly positioned where he could knock you over if something unexpectedly spooked him, so there is a trust factor on your part that this will not happen. And lastly, it is more difficult to get your horse to shift his weight to his hindquarters when you are turning away from him.

But, as with all the other activities, it is important to be equally adept from both the left and right sides of your horse. If you and your partner can lead a simple pattern with you on the left, you should be able to do so from the right as well. This is especially true with a turn on the hindquarters to the left, so leading from the right side should be your first option when attempting this turn.

After negotiating a turn on the hindquarters to the left from the right side, switch back to leading from the left. Remember that this is a very difficult turn to master from the left, so be patient with yourself and with your horse. From the left, try the corner-of-the-fence method first. Ask for a half step backward with the right front leg, then turn and take a step that is both back and to the left. After much practice, you should be turning nicely and on your way.

WITHOUT THE HALTER

If you and your partner are really working together as a team, you do not need standard control tools, such as a halter or a lead rope. Performing the above activities without any tack is a good test of your strengths and weaknesses and is also an indicator of how well you and your partner are working together. You've done some basic leading without the halter before, but now you will incorporate patterns and obstacles.

As you begin, be sure you are in an enclosed area with no grass, and no other horses present. Grass can be too tempting, or your horse may decide he is bored in the middle of a session and inappropriately decide to visit a friend being ridden at the other end of the arena.

Prior to removing the halter completely, you might try the activities with the halter on and the lead rope thrown over your partner's neck. That way you can each get used to working without the safety net a halter and lead provide, but still have the reassurance of the equipment being there if you need it. This transitional phase also accustoms you both to working without any pressure being placed on the halter, as you will not be holding onto the lead.

Begin by holding your hands as if you were actually holding the lead rope. Positioning your hands in this manner is a security blanket that is helpful now, but one you will not need for long. With your hands mimicking the normal leading position, your horse may not realize that

If you and your partner are truly working as a team, you should not need a halter or a lead rope. Here, Nomo is relaxed as she weaves through the cones and keeps herself in the correct leading position.

you do not actually have the lead rope in your hands. If, as you progress, your partner needs a little help or correction, you can reach up to briefly guide her with the halter, before resuming leading her without. If a lot of correction is needed, consider revisiting the earlier exercises with the halter and lead, and continuing those until you and your partner have more confidence.

When you can perform a simple pattern from both sides with your hands in place but not touching the halter, then drop your hands to a normal walking position. Depending on how visual your partner is, he may be confused at first by your new arm and hand position, but should quickly catch on.

Finally, remove the halter and lead. Use a confident tone of voice and body posture as you ask your friend to accompany you through the patterns and obstacles. Most likely, you will be amazed at what the two of you have just accomplished.

RESULTS!

By the time you and your horse can walk, trot, turn, and stop correctly with no behavioral issues, he should confidently follow you anywhere. You will be able to quickly stop, start, and move left and right, just as if you were dancing with a partner. This unquestioning trust that your partner now has in your leading abilities will be of help when you begin leading your friend places he does not want to go, such as into the trailer or vet stall, or through a dark barn aisle. You will also have discovered some very refined signals your horse is giving you that help you decipher his mood, and what he is thinking. This closeness will become even more evident as you move into the later activities.

A WALK IN THE PARK

Since beginning My Horse, My Partner, you and your equine friend have been working in three areas. The first has had to do with desensitization, and familiarizing your partner with a wide variety of objects, movement, and sound. The second has been to upgrade your partner's traditional groundwork abilities such as leading, longeing, and response to voice cues. And the third has been to learn to recognize your friend's likes and dislikes, and understand his or her unique signs of eagerness, distress, interest, confusion, anger, and other moods so you can better work together as a team. You have worked hard to immerse yourself and your friend in each of the above elements separately. This next activity is the first to tie all three together by combining leading and pattern work with toolkit items, desensitization, and teamwork.

Remember that to your equine partner, familiarity is everything. Even though she fully accepts you shaking bells by her ears in the comfort of her paddock, and even though you can quietly lead her on the trail behind your farm, it does not necessarily follow that your equine friend will accept being led on the trail while you are shaking bells. The way a horse's brain pigeonholes information means that when familiar activities are combined, a horse does not always recognize the two individual actions that make up the new activity. Your partner may then look at this new combination of activities as just that: New.

I once campaigned a tall Appaloosa gelding who was fine with music, fine with large indoor arenas, and fine with the rustle and bustle of people sitting in the seats of indoor arenas. But adding all of those things together made him extremely nervous. If we were in an indoor arena with music playing that was fine, but add people and he became nervous. Or, being in an indoor arena with a lot of people was okay as long as no music was playing. Obviously the combined echo or vibration of the people and the music made him uncomfortable. To help him, I spent hours standing with him in the center of huge indoor arenas during warm-up sessions at horse shows, hoping that more time in the conditions that made him antsy would make him less so. And it did. I can't say he ever felt fully comfortable with that specific combination of elements, but he improved enough to stay focused and be competitive at national-level competitions.

The moral of this story is: just like when you are introducing individual objects, with two or more objects or activities you have to repeat, repeat, repeat. You also have to be very patient.

Be Kind to Other Horses and Riders

Before combining leading with your toolkit items, be sure you are not disrupting other horses and riders. Just because your equine partner is now bored by pom-poms does not mean that they bore the horse across the arena from you. In fact, he may think that a pom-pom is the scariest thing he has ever seen and decide to run for the hills. So if other horses and horse people are present, always explain what you will be doing and ask permission to proceed in their presence. If others are uncomfortable, just go out of sight around the corner of the barn, or find another area or a different time.

Because of the extensive desensitization and partnering activities you and your horse have recently been doing, she has become more stable, more confident, and more trusting. Sometimes it is easy to forget that other horses are not equally so. Consequently, whenever you are waving plastic, tossing balls, or making odd noises around other people's horses, please keep their safety and well-being foremost in your mind.

CHOOSE FAMILIARITY FIRST

When first beginning to combine elements and activities, choose items your partner likes and is very comfortable with. For example, if you know your equine friend prefers black plastic to clear, white, or another color, you could lead her out to the pasture while slapping black plastic against your thigh, or raising the plastic over your head and shaking it. Remember that overhand movements are more threatening than other kinds of arm movements, so go slowly at first when performing these. Bear in mind that the intent is never to scare, just to interest your horse and hope that one day she will be so accustomed to it all that she will think of these new objects and actions as part of everyday life. So only go as fast—or as slow—as she tells you she is comfortable.

If your equine friend prefers green objects over those that are, for example, red, find a green plastic bag or a green pom-pom to shake while leading. You can also add music to the mix. Strap on a portable MP3 player, iPod, or CD player and turn on the style of music your horse likes best.

GETTING STARTED

Depending on the list of your horse's favorite things, some combinations to begin with could include leading through a paddock while carrying a dressage whip with a plastic bag tied to the end. You can carry the whip in front of you, angle it up or down, or hold it above your head. Make note of which position your horse accepts most readily, and which she doesn't. Here you will draw from earlier activities to ensure your body posture is relaxed and your facial expression is pleasant. This reassures your partner that there is nothing to fear.

As you walk along, you will find that the bag rustles with the rhythm of your walk. Once your partner is at ease with the situation, you can accentuate the rustle and movement of the whip and bag. Keep in mind how important rhythm is to your horse and maintain one that is very steady as you walk along.

When you and your partner are doing well with this as a team, try trotting, turning, stopping, and backing. Go back to the patterns you practiced and do some serpentines and figure eights. Walk over poles or a bridge. While you are keeping track of straight lines and round

Familiarity

Besides showing consideration for your partner, choosing familiar objects and items your horse has shown a preference for speeds the acceptance process along. Here's why: When you combine objects, your partner looks upon the combination as one new object. Your equine friend's brain then has to process every part of every element you add for sight, smell, movement, sound, and possibly taste. Then the brain has to find something familiar about the object in its data bank and determine whether or not it poses a threat. If the object is found to be familiar, your partner's brain can more quickly categorize it. Finally, all external elements such as weather, the reactions of nearby horses, your body language, even the smell of a nearby dumpster will be added to the evaluation. Only then will she decide to accept the combined object and activity, or not.

When Lucky first began walking next to me while I was carrying an umbrella, he was not at all sure about it. Even though he had previously been introduced to an umbrella in the safety of the round pen and had accepted the object, Lucky walked with his neck curved away from me so he could get a better look at this new thing that was walking with him. I say walked, but in actuality Lucky tiptoed very gingerly, head high, ready to jump at any indication of the umbrella's pending attack. But after tiptoeing for a few minutes in a small pasture, Lucky gave a huge sigh, lowered his head, relaxed his taut body, and began licking his lips. In that instant, I knew Lucky's brain had temporarily placed this object and this situation in the "odd but safe" department.

I say temporarily, because it will take repeated sessions for Lucky to permanently categorize the umbrella and the action of walking with it as a completely normal thing to do. Again, repetition comes into play.

After walking back and forth between pastures and around a field for a few minutes, Lucky is relaxed and happy.

circles, remember to keep one eye on your horse. What is it about the whip and bag combo that she is struggling with? What comes easy to her? Then determine how you can best help her through the areas that are tougher for her, such as walking over a raised pole with the bag over her head. Remember also that a little praise for a job well done can go a long, long way.

A THINKING PARTNER

Because your partner sees each combination as something brand new, it is important to put together as many of the activities and toolkit items as you can think of. The more safe and positive references your equine friend can store away in her brain, the more stable she will become, especially in unexpected situations.

Think of yourself in a fearful situation; let's say a near-miss car accident. Were you thinking how cool the car that almost hit you looked? Were you wondering how the wheels turned or how the blinkers worked? Did you accurately count the number of people inside the car or see the license plate? The answer to all of those questions most likely is, of course not! You were trying to get out of the way, get your heart to stop thumping and your hands to stop sweating, and pull off the road so you could catch your breath.

When your horse becomes fearful of something, she feels the same way. But once she has accepted an object and the fear is gone, she begins to observe the situation, and you, more closely. When your friend finally accepts, for example, a pom-pom tied to a dressage whip, she will think of the object not as a big, fluttery, scary thing, but as an object of interest. She will notice the pom-pom moves faster and the dressage whip bends more when it is windy. She will notice the interesting patterns streamers in the pom-pom make as they move through the air. She may even find them pretty. She may decide she likes the touch the pom-poms provide or the breeze they make when it is hot. This difference in perception from fear to thinking will stimulate your partner's mind. In short, the more experiences your horse has, the more curious and intelligent she can become.

Once she starts thinking, your equine friend may realize that when you come to ride you wear black boots and a specific pair of breeches or jeans. When you come to groom or feed, you may be wear-

Lucky's concern about walking with the bells is evident in his ears and body position.

ing muck boots and shorts. She knows exactly what the different attire means and reacts accordingly. She may also eventually realize that orange cones mean bending work and that the pink beach ball hanging from the fence is actually quite interesting.

ODD COMBOS

Once you realize that introducing odd combinations helps your partner think by adding experiences and references into her brain's data bank, you can get fairly creative with the process. One idea is to roll a big ball with your left hand while also holding a piece of plastic. This gives a very unusual mix of movement and sound. When you add walking or trotting, it adds even more for your friend to process.

Another is to tie a stuffed animal to the end of a longe line and bob it in front of you as you walk and trot a pattern. Blow a whistle as you skip a figure eight, or walk a reining or dressage pattern as you bounce a small ball in a tin pot. Wear a funny hat with streamers or bells on it while you feed or groom. Wave a streamer as you work a trail course from the ground. Shake a plastic bag filled with old pots and pans while you groom. The possibilities are endless.

Strange clothes are an interesting addition to the mix. Try a pattern while wearing a rain poncho or a slicker. Then experiment with carrying bells or another sound object. Or, you could try wearing a clown nose, funny glasses, and a long duster while carrying an umbrella.

Each combination may take minutes or months for your horse to process. Just remember to let your partner fully explore each new object and introduce new items to her in the now familiar routine of rubbing, then lightly tossing along her body. If you take time, you will learn to enjoy watching your partner work things out in her mind as you await acceptance.

SOCCER AND OTHER GAMES

Playing soccer and other games with your partner can be fun, team-building exercises that develop many skills. But before starting anything that involves kicking a ball, try a few practice kicks without your partner. Depending on the type of ball and the slope, type, and hardness of the terrain, even a small kick could send a ball flying. Also know that to some horses, kicking a ball (like the overhand arm movement) can seem like an act of violence. So start with small, soft nudges and be sure you have some directional skills in controlling the ball before you bring your equine partner on board.

To practice with your horse, walk along a familiar path and slowly kick the ball in front of you. Your body posture and facial expression are key here because your partner will be using them to gauge any danger in the situation. A typical initial reaction is for your partner to startle every time you kick the ball, for three reasons:

1. The kick disrupts the comforting rhythm of your walk.

2. When you are walking with the ball by your feet, the ball is in an area that is difficult for your equine partner to see. (Out of sight, out of mind.)

3. When the kicked ball suddenly shoots into your partner's line of vision, it may take a second or two for her to identify what it is, even though you've been kicking the ball for ten minutes.

Be patient, as it may take several sessions for your friend to relax and accept this process.

Think of the soccer you and your equine partner play as more of a challenge in achieving personal bests, rather than as performing against another team. Try kicking the ball through a pattern, or while trotting, turning, stopping, backing, and walking over things. See if you can kick a ball past a goal in exactly ten kicks, or five, or twelve. Challenge yourself to kick a straight twenty-foot line, or a perfect twenty-meter circle at the trot. Your partner should follow your every movement, stopping, starting, and turning exactly when you do.

This form of soccer is also an excellent activity for those who practice showmanship at halter. This activity forces quick changes in direction and speed, and gives lots of opportunity to work with a partner on setting up squarely, as you can square up by stopping with your horse's legs evenly spaced underneath herself every time the ball stops. If you keep the ball in motion through a simple pattern, no squaring is required. It is a lot of fun, and actually requires great skill to do well. Variations can include rolling a hula hoop or tossing a Frisbee instead of kicking a ball. Or, you can throw a small lightweight ball into specific target areas, or "bowl" your way through a pattern.

Lucky is more interested in the man behind the camera than in walking with the ball—a great sign!

Remember, though, that this is a challenge for the two of you as a team. Never, ever go past the comfort level of your equine partner. You will know what that level is, because she will tell you—and you will be listening. Slowly, over time, you will both increase your confidence and skills. Understand that the hesitancy your horse shows may be a trust issue. She isn't sure you can handle the ball nearly as well as you think you can. And you know what? She may be right! She wants to be absolutely sure that you do not inadvertently kick the ball into her face or legs. She also wants to be sure that her clumsy, two-footed partner does not trip over the ball or fall where she might step on you.

Think also about the color of the ball you are using. A light-colored soccer ball does not provide much contrast on a sandy surface. Be sure there is enough difference in color that your horse can clearly see the ball. Larger balls roll slower and are easier for your partner to see, so consider one of those. For more advanced work, try a ball that lights up, glows as it rolls, or makes some kind of noise. But these are only for after you have built up a comfort level, confidence, and trust in each other with the initial activities.

From the Horse's Perspective

Something happens when you take your friend on a trip that is similar to the excitement of a child going to a candy store, or for ice cream. New sights, sounds, and smells completely distract your partner. Take time, however, to see your new surroundings through the eyes of your horse.

- Put yourself at her eye level and look around, paying special attention to shadows, contrasts, flags, or other items flying in the wind.
- Then listen. What do you hear? Remember that your horse will hear far more than you do, but can you hear the distant rumble of a train? Is there noise from a nearby highway or factory?
- Finally, what can you smell? A dumpster? A pond? Fresh manure from other horses?

Experiencing a new environment from your partner's perspective will help you anticipate areas of the grounds that might make your horse uncomfortable, and identify other areas where she will feel more relaxed.

NEW LOCATIONS

By now, you can put together a number of unusual combinations of leading and toolkit items and can work well together on familiar ground. The real test comes when you can do the same thing with the same positive results away from home.

Depending on your setup, you might not be able to take your horse off property. In that case, locate an obscure area of your farm or an area your equine friend does not normally visit. If you can take a little trip, a park that has horse trails, a friend's barn, or a horse-show grounds (especially if you can get in on a non-show day) are all good options.

If your equine friend is a little excited in the new location, spend a few minutes longeing her. This allows her to burn off excess energy and have a more focused mindset when you begin work as a team. As always, start slow. I do not like to go into off-site activities with any preconceived ideas of what can be accomplished. Start with very early activities, such as rubbing your equine friend with a plastic bag, and progress from there to lightly tossing the bag along both sides of her body. You also want to be sure she is responding to the whoa cue, so bring a chain to attach to your lead rope in case a reminder session is needed. Chances are, though, that you will not have to use it.

Ideally, you and your horse will be able to progress to some of the activities in this chapter, but that may not be possible, especially the first few times away from home. Horses who have been campaigned at horse shows, or taken on trail rides from an early age, process new locations much better than those who rarely leave the farm. So if your partner has been homebound for some time, a little trip will be especially exciting to her. Use the first outing as a baseline, then try on each successive outing to get one step further. Over time, you will make progress, and eventually you and your equine friend will work together as a team just as well away from home as you do in your own backyard.

RESULTS!

A few years ago a friend of mine was trying to catch her horse during an unexpected sleet storm. Ice patches were quickly forming and she was afraid her gelding, who was recovering from a tendon injury, would skid on the ice and re-injure himself. To protect herself from the stinging ice pellets that were falling from the sky, my friend put on her slicker, but the gelding, who clearly wanted to come in, was terrified of the bright red vinyl figure who had entered his pasture. My friend eventually gave up and took the slicker off, but by then the gelding was so worked up, he just wanted to be left alone. He stayed out during the storm and fortunately weathered it well, but both he and his human partner would have been happier had he allowed the slicker-clad woman to lead him in from the squall.

Leading and performing pattern work while doing odd activities and wearing odd clothing can help your partner in many such circumstances. The more exposure to things that are very different, the more entries your partner will have in the data bank that is her brain. If the entries are categorized as "safe," then your partner will calmly accept the most unusual of circumstances. Combination work is simply another step in making the unique routine.

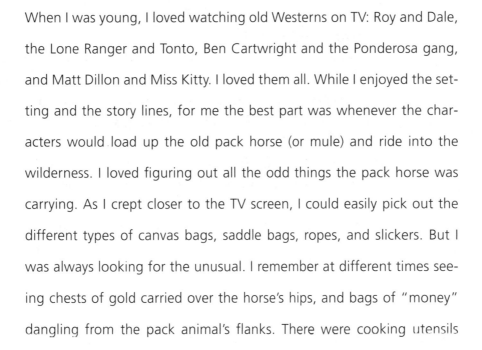

HANG ONE

When I was young, I loved watching old Westerns on TV: Roy and Dale, the Lone Ranger and Tonto, Ben Cartwright and the Ponderosa gang, and Matt Dillon and Miss Kitty. I loved them all. While I enjoyed the setting and the story lines, for me the best part was whenever the characters would load up the old pack horse (or mule) and ride into the wilderness. I loved figuring out all the odd things the pack horse was carrying. As I crept closer to the TV screen, I could easily pick out the different types of canvas bags, saddle bags, ropes, and slickers. But I was always looking for the unusual. I remember at different times seeing chests of gold carried over the horse's hips, and bags of "money" dangling from the pack animal's flanks. There were cooking utensils hanging all over one horse, and in one episode a newborn calf rode on the back of a draft mule.

While the average horse today will never have to carry a calf back to the homestead, it isn't far-fetched to think a rider would need to put on a slicker during a rainy trail ride, or while waiting to compete at an event. A horse today might need to help carry duffel bags from the trailer to the barn, or remain steady when the wind sends a paper bag tumbling through the middle of a three-day event. Being prepared for

131

the unexpected isn't just a matter of practicality; it can mean the difference between a minor incident and a major accident, or a blue ribbon and the gate.

The big distinction between this next activity and the ones preceding it is that up to now, your partner could, if he desired, choose to move away from an object. But like the pack horses of the Old West, you will begin hanging the now familiar toolkit items on your equine partner, which means your partner will not be able to step away from an object. To accomplish this successfully, both of you need high levels of trust and confidence in each other.

EQUIPMENT

Before starting, let's take a moment to discuss the tack from which you will be hanging the items. You will need either a saddle or a surcingle; I encourage you not to use your best show-ring tack. If you do not have a surcingle or an old saddle lying around, try hooking two girths together to fit like a surcingle.

Whatever equipment you use, it must fit well. If your equine friend's saddle does not fit him, he will be uncomfortable enough that he cannot focus on doing his job. Think of yourself going to work every day in a pair of shoes that are a size too large, or a jacket that is

Saddle Condition

Before you ever place a saddle on your horse's back, it is important to check its condition. Be sure all stitching is tight and in place, and that the leather or synthetic material is in good repair.

Then put the pommel (the front of the saddle) down on a pad or protective piece of carpeting with the back sticking up. Look down the seat of the saddle. Is there a straight line from the center of the cantle (the back of the saddle) along the seat to the center of the pommel? Or

is there a twist? If there is a twist it could mean an uneven or a broken tree, which will be both uncomfortable and unsafe for both you and your equine friend.

Lastly, place the cantle on your hip and pull steadily on the pommel. If wrinkles appear in the seat, this could be another sign that the tree is damaged. If this is the case, have an expert take a look at it.

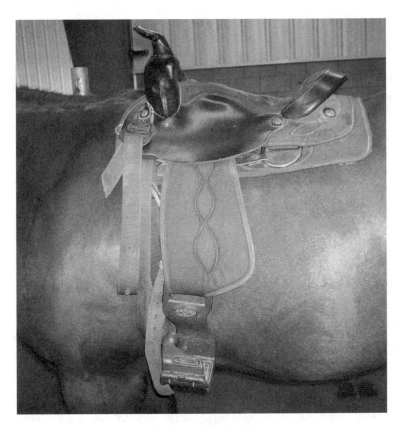

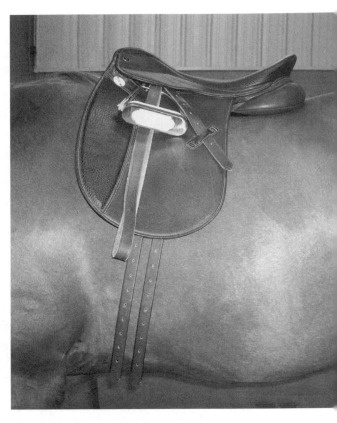

two sizes too small. At the very least, the poor fit is distracting, and may eventually become painful.

FITTING A SADDLE

Fitting a saddle to your horse is not difficult, although the number of saddles out there that do not seem to fit any horse is amazing. Like many non-profit groups that are involved in equine-assisted activities, Saddle Up! often receives generous donations of used saddles. But even with a herd of more than twenty horses of all breeds, sizes, and shapes, some saddles (even some that are very well made) do not fit any of the Saddle Up! horses. Saddle (or surcingle) fit is crucial, so before proceeding, use the basic checklist that follows to be sure the saddle you are using on your equine friend fits comfortably. Even though Western and English saddles look very different, the checklist for fitting either type of saddle is similar.

Assuming the saddle checks out well, the next step is to place the saddle on your horse's back without benefit of any pads. Pads can mask the true fit of a saddle, so it is easier to check the fit without

LEFT: This Western saddle fits Nelson nicely. It has a level seat and good clearance in the front, does not pinch or dig in at the back, and does not bridge along the sides.

RIGHT: This English saddle does not fit Nelson very well. It sits too high on his withers, indicating that it is tight in the shoulders. The seat tips back, which will keep a rider perpetually off balance. And under the seat, along the sides, the saddle bridges, creating a gap between saddle and horse. This saddle would do much better on a horse with a narrower build.

them. Also, do not worry about doing up the cinch or girth. Instead, just let the saddle sit on your horse's back. To check the fit:

1. You should be able to stick three fingers into the opening between your equine friend's withers and the front of the saddle. If you can't, the saddle sits too low on your partner's back. The exception here is an English cutback saddle, which leaves the withers open.

2. If you look at the saddle from the side, the seat should be level. If it is tilting forward or backward, the saddle will pitch the rider in the same direction. Some leveling can be done with a "bump" pad, but ideally, the saddle's seat should be level.

3. Make your hand flat, and stick your fingers in as far as you can between the front of the saddle and your horse's shoulder. Start at the top where the saddle first makes contact with your partner and run your hand all the way down. If at any point your feel a lot of pressure or pinching, the saddle is too tight for your friend.

4. Look under the saddle where your knee would lie, and also behind the thigh area. Does the saddle fit nicely along your horse's side, or does it stick out and form a gap? If there is a gap, the saddle is probably too wide; it will not provide enough support to stay in place and may tip or rock.

5. Under where your hips would be on the sides, the saddle should also fit snugly with no gaps or "bridging," and also no undue tightness.

6. The back of the saddle should neither dig into the horse's spine (which many Western saddles do), or tip up so there is no contact (typical of English saddles). With an English saddle, you should also be able to see daylight all the way through the gullet, or underside of the saddle, along the horse's spine.

7. Like everything else, be sure to check the fit on both the left and right sides. Over time and depending on his job, a horse can build up more muscle on one side of his body than on the other. This means that a specific saddle might fit on the left side, but

not on the right, or vice versa. To fit correctly, a saddle must fit the horse well on both sides.

FITTING A SURCINGLE

A surcingle is a wide (and usually padded) strap that fits snugly around your partner's girth area. Many surcingles have a number of strategically placed hooks or metal loops, through which longe lines or driving reins can be run, and that are excellent for hanging things on as well. Surcingles are much less complicated to fit than saddles, but the fit is no less important. If parts of the surcingle are digging into your partner's back, or if it pinches him in the girth area, he will not be able to do his best for you. Regular longeing surcingles fit most horses, but it is always a good idea to check the fit, just in case your horse and your surcingle are not a good match.

To check the fit, place the surcingle on your partner's back without a pad and see how it lies. If you buckle the girth, are there areas that gap or bulge? Do you see parts that dig into your friend? Does it fit smoothly across his topline? Chances are that your surcingle does fit well. If not, try two girths or cinches buckled together, but they, too, must fit comfortably around your horse.

BIT CLIPS AND LADDER REINS

In Chapter One, bit clips and ladder reins were briefly mentioned as items needed for your toolkit. You are almost ready to use them. Bit clips will be used to attach objects to your partner's saddle or surcingle, and ladder reins provide an opportunity to attach items that will dangle on your partner's flank and over his tail.

TAKE STOCK

Before moving on to this next activity, know that most horse/human relationships do not come anywhere close to what you have already developed with your partner. What you have now is a very unique and special understanding of each other. But to fully appreciate the relationship and what you have accomplished, it is important to take time to do a quick review of how far the two of you have come together. How many new things have you discovered about your favorite equine? What colors does he like best? What kinds of music

Nelson stands quietly but alertly as a plastic bag hangs from his surcingle.

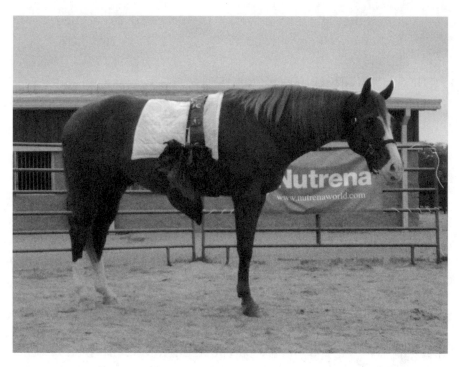

are relaxing to him? What signals does he give you when he is bored, nervous or interested? What activities have been easy for you as a team? What has been especially difficult for you or for him? What recent accomplishment are you most proud of? What has been disappointing?

Taking stock of your progress shows just how far you have traveled. It points out your strengths and weaknesses as a team and as individuals, and lets you know what to expect in upcoming activities. For example, if your partner still struggles with being led from the right side, plan to spend more time and be more patient when working from the right. If you have difficulty finding a rhythm in desensitization work, you know you need to practice longer with the item to become more at ease with it before introducing it to your horse.

Several things with which your partner should be very comfortable by now are the staples of your toolkit: pom-poms, bells, plastic, stuffed animals, and so on. One reason he has become comfortable is that he has always had the option to move away from an item he is not sure about. Moving away from an object gives your partner a little breathing room in which he can assess the object from a distance. That is about to change. By now the trust and confidence levels you both have in each other should be sufficient enough to allow you to hang a familiar object from a saddle or surcingle while is it on your equine friend.

HANG ONE ITEM

Hanging an object is a real milestone for you both. You have to trust that your horse will act sensibly, even if he is uncertain, and he has to trust that you will not expose him to anything dangerous. With that trust comes confidence in yourself and in your partner.

Begin in a safe enclosure, such as a round pen or small paddock. Tack up your partner with a halter and a saddle or a surcingle, and then choose a comfortable and familiar item. It could be an empty paper or plastic bag, a pom-pom, or even a stuffed toy. Then clip the item to your partner's saddle or surcingle. The item should dangle near where your foot would be if you were riding him, but not so low that it interferes with your horse's movement. Additionally, the item should not be one that is uncomfortable for your equine friend to wear, such as a hard plastic toy that could bump his elbow, or a heavy bucket that bangs his ribs.

Now move away to leave your horse free to inspect the object, play with it, and gradually learn to move with it. As in earlier activities, let him figure out for himself that this object, while attached to him, is not a threat. A horse will typically try to move sideways, away from the object, but should not become overly concerned when he realizes that no matter where he moves, the object moves with him. After all, whatever is clipped to his side is something he has spent a great deal of time with recently.

If your friend becomes overly anxious or frightened, just step into his line of vision and talk to him. Your presence and voice should be enough to calm him. If he is upset enough to cause himself harm, then you can simply unsnap the object and try again later, after he has quieted down.

LEFT AND RIGHT

Once your equine friend has become comfortable with the object clipped to his left side, then try the same item on the right. Be sure to clip the item in the same place on the right side as you did on the left. By now your horse should be reasonably well-versed on both his left and right sides, but it is still important to introduce every new concept on both sides so each side of his brain recognizes it as something safe.

Again, you can watch from an inconspicuous place, but basically leave him alone to figure it out.

MOVING FORWARD

Many horses will appear to accept an object that is clipped to them because they are quietly standing still. The head can be lowered, the lips moving, and the ears relaxed, but these horses are only comfortable with the object because they are not moving.

Lucky is one such horse. Whenever a new item is introduced to him, he is very agreeable . . . until you ask him to move. Then Lucky becomes quite concerned. He first turns to his human partner for help. When his partner encourages him to move forward, he does so very tentatively, moving tensely, ears back, head up and sideways toward the object, lips tight. But after a few minutes of moving at the walk and trot, he visibly relaxes, his head lowers and comes around in front of him, his ears start to swivel, and he begins licking and chewing. Lucky is very predictable, as he goes through this same process every time he encounters something new.

Your horse has his own process, which by now you should recognize very well. When first asking him to move forward, let him move freely if at all possible. If he can freely walk or trot around a round pen or paddock, he will be more comfortable than if you are longeing him. If he is moving about freely, he has complete control over his body and his actions, and this control makes him feel safe.

You want to persuade him to move, but not to race wildly about. So depending on your horse, you may need a longe whip to encourage forward motion, or you may need to use body position and language to ask him to settle down. Remember that stepping forward of his center will make him slow down, and staying behind will cause him to move forward. In either case, your relaxed body and pleasant facial expression will help your partner feel safe and confident.

LEADING AND LONGEING

When your partner moves freely with the object on his left and his right side, you can then ask him to lead through a pattern, or around

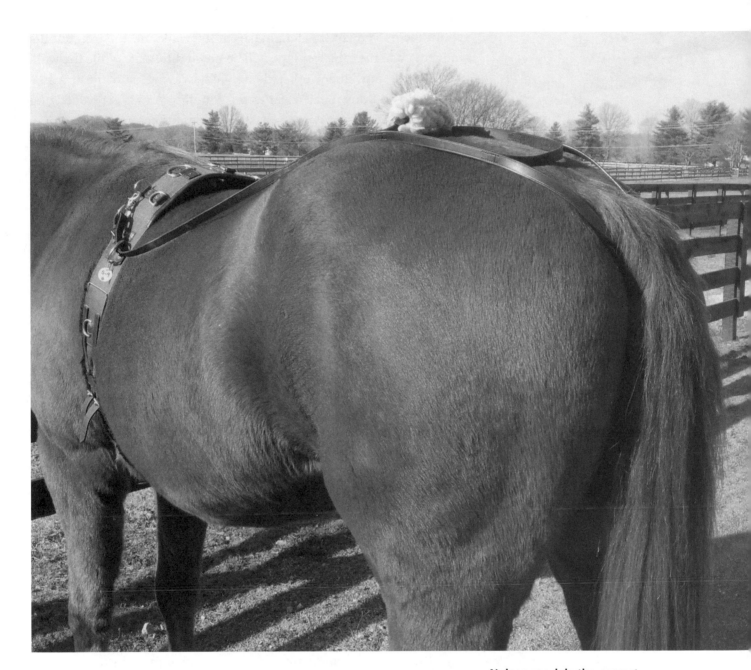

your barn. His favorite music or the sound of your voice will help get rid of any lingering anxiety about the item that is still hanging from his side. Be sure to lead at the walk and trot from both the left and right sides, and with the item on each side, as well.

When you are leading well as a team, you and your partner can move to the longeing stage. Begin at the walk and only move to the trot when you have his attention. Your horse should be very relaxed

Nelson models the correct fit of ladder reins: not too tight or too loose under the tail, with excess reins run through a lower loop on the surcingle, then attached to a higher loop.

about the movement the item makes at the walk and the trot, but the movement at the canter or lope will be much different. While the walk causes little movement other than some swaying, and the trot is a mostly up-and-down gait as far as the dangling item is concerned, the canter or lope can really get a plastic bag or stuffed animal swinging. Your partner may catch its movement out of the corner of his eye that startles him, or it may brush against his sides in a different way. You can always bring him down to a more comfortable walk or trot for a minute and try again. Repetition and patience can work wonders.

ALTERNATE LOCATIONS

When your partner is comfortable with the object hanging on both his left and right sides, you can add ladder reins to the mix. The ends of the ladder reins that normally fasten to the bit will, for this use, be clipped to two of the metal loops on the surcingle or saddle. Then run the ladder part of the reins over the top of your partner's back and buckle the middle of the reins under his tail, like a crupper.

The fit of the ladder reins is crucial, as you do not want them to be too tight, which would pull on the tail and be uncomfortable for your friend. If they are too loose, they and the item attached to them will slide to one side, also creating pressure on his tail. It helps to anchor the end that is normally attached to the bit low, near the girth. If the reins are still too long and hang down under the tail, run the reins through a lower loop then attach them to a higher loop. Ideally, there should be about two inches of slack between the tail and the closed end of the ladder reins.

If your partner is a trail, driving, or ranch horse, or if he has very flat withers, he may have worn a crupper before and will quickly get used to the ladder reins. If not, give him enough time to decide that this strange contraption over his back and under his tail is non-threatening. Then repeat the process you went through when you hung the object from your horse: turn him loose in a small area, then lead him in patterns, and finally longe.

When he is comfortable with the ladder reins, take the object you originally hung, and hang it from the reins over his croup. You know the drill. Turn him loose in a small area, lead patterns, and longe. Hang from the other side and repeat.

Remember that a horse's brain works differently than a human brain. You might say, "Why don't I just put the ladder reins on and hang stuff?" That might work for you, but it will not work for your horse. You have to deal with him on his level in a way that he understands. To your partner, every change you make is a new concept. Hanging the same item so it falls over his hips rather than over his shoulder, to him, is different. It sounds like a long, slow process, and honestly, it can be. But most horses progress relatively quickly as long as you introduce each step separately. You are developing the foundation for a lifelong relationship with this horse, and that cannot come in a matter of days, or even months.

Another area to hang from is the top of the tail. You can do this by using the last rung on the ladder reins and centering the object over the tail. I took Lucky on a trail ride a few months ago when he somehow got a huge, bushy branch with a lot of dead leaves stuck in his tail. This branch was about three feet high, four across, and five long. Lucky pulled this very unwieldy branch calmly at a walk for a few hundred feet while it hit his back legs at every step. We were on a very narrow trail on a downhill slope where there was not a lot of room to dismount, but I could see a clearing up ahead. I have ridden many other horses who would have panicked, but Lucky had just spent much of the previous week with a paper bag hanging over his tail, and he remained very calm.

A stirrup or a low ring on the surcingle is also a good spot to hang objects. This will let the item hang down your partner's leg, but as a safety measure, make sure the lowest point of the object is still above the top of your equine friend's knee. You can also clip the item so it lies across his back.

OTHER ITEMS

As your horse becomes accustomed to one individual object, and when you can hang that object anywhere on his body and longe him in both directions at the walk, trot (or equivalent gait), and canter, you can exchange it for another item, but only use one object at a time at this stage. Repeat the process until as many of the toolkit items as possible have been individually tied to your partner.

Be sure to stay away from anything that might bump or bang, or anything with sharp points or that is heavy. Bags, pom-poms, plastic, towels, stuffed animals, and plastic or foam rubber balls are all good to use.

RESULTS!

Remember that there is a real possibility that when you and your partner are riding, you will need to put a windbreaker on (or take one off), and the sleeves could easily brush his sides in the process. Or, a piece of plastic could blow up against him when you are leading him to the pasture, or your hat could blow off and land on his rump. Everything you are doing now will help turn those unexpected, scary, and potentially harmful incidents into non-events.

Even though you may not have realized it, the repetitive process has helped you as much as it has your equine friend, by solidifying his behaviors in your mind and giving you extra practice for activities yet to come.

DRIVING UNDER THE INFLUENCE

While longeing has its uses, it also has limitations. Longeing is excellent for conditioning; for letting your friend burn off excess energy before a session on the ground or under saddle; for teaching voice cues; and for building respect, confidence, and trust. It is also a wonderful tool for desensitization work, and for getting your partner accustomed to new objects. But there is a more advanced process that will teach you and your equine friend much more: long lining.

Long lining allows the human partner to add direction, balance, and collection to the horse's movement from the ground. The differences between longeing and long lining are simple. Long lining uses a bridle instead of a halter. And instead of one longe line attached to the halter, there are two long lines attached to the bit.

The process also builds new levels of trust and confidence as the human partner slowly moves from alongside the horse to behind, and begins to use the principles in long lining to actually drive the horse from the ground. While the change is a simple matter of positioning, it means the equine partner can no longer see her human friend. This lack of visibility requires the horse to have a great deal of confidence, and to be fully attuned to both verbal and rein cues.

Building Confidence with Long Lining

Many years ago, a stunning bay Arabian gelding was brought to me for help. Eban needed to compete in 4-H trail classes but had developed a fear of tarps, which was a class requirement. Eban would go over a tarp just fine if he were led over it, because he had a human partner alongside him that he could look to for confirmation. If his human partner was going over the tarp, he reasoned, then it must be okay.

But Eban's reasoning did not extend to walking over a tarp with a rider on his back. That was another matter. With a rider, Eban did not have the visual affirmation he needed of a strong and relaxed human to let him know the obstacle was safe. At this point in his life, Eban was not a very confident horse.

I tried longeing Eban over the obstacle, but the halter and lead did not give me as much control as I needed, and he began ducking around the tarp or reversing directions. But when I began long lining him over the tarp, the safety of seeing me in the center of the circle, combined with the traditional riding aids of bit and reins, gave him enough confidence and encouragement to hesitantly begin to cross it. When he became fully comfortable with the idea of walking over the tarp with me at longeing distance, I used his newfound confidence to move onto his back. Soon after, Eban was reunited with his owner and was enjoying the trail class he so recently had feared.

Some time later, Eban's owner brought him back to me for help with an additional problem. She had moved up to breed shows and was campaigning him in non-pro showmanship classes. While the two worked very well as a team, she felt Eban's lack of presence, that "it factor" that so many great horses have, kept her in the lower placings. After re-evaluating the horse, I felt Eban's problem was really a lack of confidence, of boldness, in himself.

I built on the previous long-line training and began ground driving Eban around the farm. We drove up and down hills, through trees, and around and over obstacles. Eban had to learn to trust himself, because when I was standing behind him in the driving position, he usually could not see me. As his training level grew so did his confidence, and it showed in the way he walked, the way he held himself, and even in the way he related to other horses. Eban was no longer the bottom horse in the herd. He never became a dominant horse, but ground driving helped Eban build enough confidence that he could hold his own in a group of horses, and he could also walk with enough pride into the show ring to help his owner earn quite a few blue ribbons.

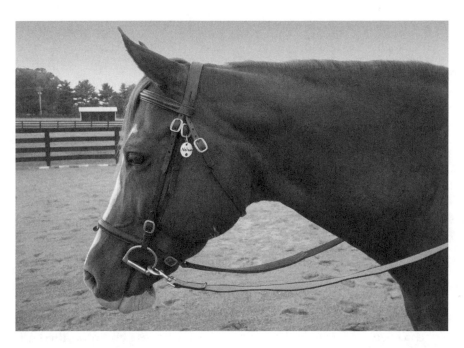

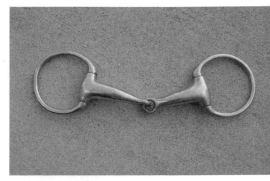

LEFT: This English bridle and D-ring snaffle fit Nelson well. The throatlatch is not too tight, the cavesson (or noseband) is snug and fits a few fingers below Nelson's cheekbone, the browband is long enough for the cheek-pieces to form a straight line from bit to poll, and the bit is placed high enough in Nelson's mouth to offer good control, but not so high that he loses comfort.

RIGHT: This mild eggbutt snaffle offers direct control from the horse's mouth to the reins. The horse feels the pull on the sides of his mouth, which works excep-tionally well for long lining and driving.

EQUIPMENT

THE BRIDLE AND BIT

The first thing you need to long line your partner is a well-fitting bri-dle with a snaffle bit. A snaffle bit is characterized by a lack of shanks, meaning that the reins attach directly to the ring at the horse's mouth and not to a bar that extends downward from that ring. I like eggbutt, full-cheek or D-ring snaffles over any kind of O-ring snaffle, as O-rings can pinch the corner of your friend's mouth.

The bridle can be English or Western and with a noseband or with-out. But it should have either a browband or split-ear headstall that al-lows the cheekpieces, or sides of the bridle, to sit well away from your partner's eyes. And it should have a throatlatch that is buckled loosely enough that you can stick your hand between it and horse's cheek. The throatlatch prevents the bridle from slipping off over your part-ner's ears. And obviously, any bridle you use should be in good repair with the stitching intact.

The bit should be wide enough so you can see about an eighth of an inch of the mouthpiece of the bit on either side of your friend's mouth. It should be positioned high enough to see a wrinkle, or maybe two, at the mouth's corners. The number of wrinkles depends on the depth of your partner's mouth. Valentino has a very shallow mouth and needs more wrinkles, or the bit will be too low and hit his teeth. Nacho has a wide, deep mouth, so the bit does not need to be placed as high in his mouth as Valentino's does.

Before using a bit for the first time, and periodically thereafter, check to ensure your friend's teeth are in good shape and that the bit you are using is not interfering with them in any way.

Another option is to use a sidepull hackamore. If your horse is not trained for a bit, this is a great alternative. Be sure, however, to stay away from bosal or mechanical hackamores. Each has its place, but they do not work well for this activity.

THE LINES

Depending on your budget and resources, you can use a pair of driving reins, which are somewhat shorter than longe lines, or you can use two longe lines. Because the longe lines are longer, they are more awkward to use, but provided that they do not have a chain on the end, they work just fine. The weight of chains on the end of longe lines can cause your friend to carry her head lower than usual, and can also swing in an annoying manner.

THE REST

You will also need a driving, dressage, or longe whip, and a saddle or surcingle. Traditionally in long lining, the lines (or reins) are run through one of several metal loops on a surcingle. As you will have to switch directions and raise the lines over your partner's back, I prefer to use a loop that is toward the top of the surcingle.

If you are using a saddle, you will have to find a place to run the lines through. With an English saddle, try attaching a bit clip to the front rings on each side of the saddle. These are the same rings you would attach a breastplate or martingale to, and are the easiest position in which to move the lines from side to side. But sometimes, depending on the height of your partner's withers and the width of the gullet, it is easier to run your stirrups up, and then run the lines through the stirrups.

With a Western saddle you may be able to run the lines through the front of the saddle under the horn, but using a ring behind the seat often works better. It's really a matter of trial and error and finding what works best for you and your horse.

GETTING STARTED

Long lining is very similar to longeing, except that you have two lines instead of one. And as with longeing, the smaller the circle, the more control you have. A good rule of thumb to begin with is to send your partner out in a circle using about half your lines. Because it can be a handful to hold one line in your left hand and the other in your right plus a longe whip, it is easier at first to work without a longe whip, if at all possible. The ends of each line should come up through the heel of your hand as it would if you were longeing. The lines should be held in a figure eight, and not dragging on the ground where you can trip over them, or coiled so they could tighten and injure your hand.

It is also important to realize that your hands are now connected to your partner's mouth. Maintain light and steady contact. You will quickly find out if you are pulling harder on one line than another, because your partner will turn in the direction you are pulling.

To begin, position yourself and your partner as you would if you were longeing, and then use your walk cue to ask your equine friend to move forward. Remember to say "walk" or "walk on" with a period at the end of the word and not a question mark. If your horse is confused or ignoring you, say "walk on" with an exclamation point on the end, and be sure to stand behind your partner's center of balance. Taking a step toward her hindquarters as you cluck or kiss to her might also help.

Nelson shows some confusion with the long-line process. He wants to turn toward his human partner for reassurance, and so the outside rein is tight. Nelson's ears and head also indicate his hesitancy.

Maintain forward movement for several laps before asking your partner to stop. Turning toward you when she stops is a natural reaction for a horse and a sign that she wants to be attentive and helpful. However, when long lining, this puts you in front of her center. And, because the lines go from the bit, through a loop near her back and then to your hand, there is no direct line from her head to your hand as there is in longeing. For those reasons, it is better if your horse understands that even though you are on the ground beside her, she needs to stop straight, as she would if you were riding her. If she were under saddle, you would not want her to turn toward the center of the ring every time she stopped. Instead, you would want her to stop straight along the rail. It is the same with long lining.

To keep her from turning toward you after halting, increase the pressure on the outside line every time she begins to turn in. Reinforce the rein cue with a firm verbal cue of "whoa," followed by an enthusiastic "good girl" when she responds correctly. After a few tries she will begin to get the idea. Then practice the walk/whoa transition both directions until each of you is comfortable and competent.

LARGER CIRCLES

Once you and your partner are working well in both directions in a mid-sized circle, let the lines play out to walk the largest circle you can. The dynamics of the larger circle mean that there is more room for error in turning, but some practice with the bigger format will take care of that.

If your horse is insecure about the process, her anxiety may grow when the larger circle places you further away from her. She could show this by stopping frequently, trying to turn to face you, wiggling her hindquarters, or not staying on the track of the circle. A raised neck, pinned ears, excessive chewing on the bit, and swishing her tail are other indications that she may be confused or uncertain. Keep sending her strong cues and encourage her with your voice and body language. Eventually you will see her relax and begin to walk with more purpose.

SPIRALS

When you have mastered the larger circle, then the two of you are ready to try spirals. Spirals are continuing and increasingly smaller circles, just like you would draw on a piece of paper. When you and your horse are walking the smallest circle you can, then you can spi-ral outward, making the circles increasingly larger until you have reached the end of the lines. Spirals help you both gain better control when long lining because you constantly have to change the pressure on the bit to direct your partner. Your partner, in responding to the cue, has to bend or unbend her body to stay on track and maintain for-ward motion.

You may find, particularly in the smaller circles, that your friend is more reluctant in one direction. This could be due to underlying soreness, or maybe her muscles have developed differently on one side. Nomo, having played polo, bends more easily to the left than she does to the right. Polo is usually played with the rider's right arm swinging the mallet, so polo ponies often travel somewhat bent to the left—away from the mallet. If your partner's reluctance is significant, consider having your veterinarian, or a local equine massage therapist or chiropractor, evaluate her.

CHANGING DIRECTIONS

Now comes the fun part: learning to change direction while maintain-ing forward motion. This can be accomplished by practicing figure eights and serpentines by asking your partner to turn away from you at the walk. To make a right turn for example, you will have to raise your arms up so the lines clear your horse's rump, while using your right rein as a guide. You may also need to loosen your left rein, which will allow your horse to turn her head in the direction you want her to go. Of course, you do not want to bump or jar her mouth in the process, so you might need to repeat the process a few times before getting it right. Also be sure you have allowed enough room for the two of you to turn. When you are first learning, the turn can use a great deal of arena space.

Depending on your height and build in relation to your partner's, turning could be awkward at first. I am five-foot-eight, and with Valentino, who is just 14.2, we have no difficulty making any number of turns on the long line. But even with my height, it is a stretch for me to maneuver Nelson, who is 16 hands. Then again, it can be difficult to turn Nacho, who is also just 14.2, but whose extreme Haflinger bulk makes up for his short stature. It can be tricky to get the lines over and around his very wide set of haunches.

THE TROT AND CANTER

Long lining at higher gaits is more difficult for you than it is for your partner. First you have to get used to the feel of the gait coming through the lines into your hands without pulling on your partner's mouth. Then there is the added speed to contend with. In changing direction, you will need to move faster than ever before. You may also need to use a longe whip, which adds to the bulk that is already in your hands.

Beyond those considerations, long lining at the trot and canter is much like longeing at higher gaits. You also need to remember that if your partner ever pulls you off balance, if for some reason you trip and fall, or if your partner becomes a little too enthusiastic, just let go. Nothing is worth you being dragged, and you are in an enclosed area so your horse can't get into too much trouble.

At the trot you can vary the speed and the size of the circle as you practice changing tracks, or direction. And it will take a little practice to coordinate the pull of the outside line, raising your hands above the croup, steadying your partner at the end of the line with the other rein, and the necessary movement of your body—all without breaking gait. Be sure to give the two of you enough room to turn; due to the increased speed, turning at the trot will take up far more space than at a walk.

You and your partner will need to be very, very skilled to do a long-line direction change at the canter. Not every team achieves this goal, or if they do, it can take many months of practice. Before attempting this move, be sure your horse is in a nice, slow, collected canter on the correct lead. When you change direction, you will need to ask for a simple lead change, which means breaking to the trot for the turn, then asking for a canter on the other lead once the turn is completed. The fewer trotting strides the two of you can do this in the better. Very advanced teams can also do a halt, a turn to the outside on the hindquarters, and then resume the canter in the other direction, but again, perfecting this move takes a great deal of time and patience. It is, however, a worthy goal.

DRIVING

As I mentioned in my story about Eban, your partner may not be able to see you when you are driving her. Your only communication will be

through your voice and your hands, and this requires a good bit of concentration, confidence, focus, and trust.

Switching to driving mode is simply a matter of positioning. Instead of standing to the side, behind your horse's center of balance, you will stand behind your partner. Be sure to stand far enough behind that you do not get caught in the natural motions of your equine friend's stride. You also want to be sure you are far enough back that if your horse suddenly stopped and backed up, or if she kicked, you would not be knocked over.

In addition to being safer, standing farther back is easier. It gives you a larger perspective and you may even be able to see your partner's head and ears, depending on the height ratios and the angle of her neck.

If you and your horse have never driven before, it is easiest to begin as you would if you were long lining her, then gradually move to a position that is behind her. Then, instead of walking a circle, ask her to walk a straight line.

After a few sessions, Nelson is able to ground drive confidently. Nelson's human partner is also far enough behind to remain safe in case of a sudden stop.

Chances are your partner will walk on as if she has been doing this all her life. Some horses, however, become confused or hesitant when you move back and drop out of the line of vision. Turning to look at you and being reluctant to move forward are typical insecure reactions. If this is the case, reassure her with your firm voice and encourage her to walk on. Note that if you are nervous, it will show in your voice and your equine friend will pick up on your unease. So only move from long lining to driving when you *both* are ready.

Walking a straight line next to an arena railing or wall is also helpful because that is something your horse is probably familiar with. When you ride, you probably spend some time on the rail, so she may feel more comfortable there. You may also need to backtrack by moving a few steps sideways into her line of vision. Then as she sees your confident body posture and gains more assurance, you can gradually step behind her.

A few horses have too much forward motion at first, and this is usually due to fear; it's the instinctive flight mechanism telling her to get away from this strange situation. Instead of turning her head to look at you, she will probably elevate it. She may rush forward until you ask her to stop, and in response she will swing her entire body around to face you. It is the opposite problem to the horse who does not want to move forward, but the solution is the same: step sideways until she can see you and proceed from there. Before too long your friend will be more confident of her abilities and you can step back behind.

Practice walking and stopping along the rail until you and your partner are comfortable with the process, with you standing behind her. The speed with which she accepts this will depend on how confident she is in herself and how much she trusts you. Remember that horses thrive on repetition. Doing the same thing over and over imprints their brains with the action, and the action eventually becomes both safe and routine.

When you have mastered the walk/whoa transition along the rail, try setting up a simple pattern for the two of you. Maybe you walk over a pole, weave through three markers, do a circle around a fourth marker, and stop. Or you could try figure eights and serpentines, reverses, walking between poles, and even a few backing steps. You will be surprised at how much you can achieve with just a few driving sessions. It's also a lot of fun!

If you are able, you can also try trotting. You will have to trot along behind, so be extra sure that the footing is good, and that your partner trots at a pace you can match. When you can trot as a team along the rail, incorporate some trotting into a pattern.

Nelson listens intently as I drive him with a Western saddle through a series of patterns and cones.

RESULTS!

Driving forces each of you to communicate in new ways. Your partner cannot see you, and you can't see much, if anything, of her ears or face. Without the visual of soft eyes, licking and chewing, swiveling ears, and a lowered head, how do you know what your horse is thinking and feeling? Well, you've got a great view of the other end of your horse. Quick swishing of her tail can mean anxiety or anger. Also watch her footfalls. Are her legs moving in a relaxed manner? Does her rump seem soft? Or tense? What do you feel through your hands? Is she tugging at the bit? Refusing to turn? Or is she responsive and re-laxed? Once you see what you *do* have to work with, you will find there are still many ways to read your horse.

But how will your partner know what you are feeling? Your voice is a good indicator. If it is both calm and strong, you can project your confidence toward her. She will also feel your steady hands. If your hands are shaking or trembling, then you will transmit your fear to her.

After a few driving sessions, something else will develop, if it hasn't already: intuition. Somehow, you will just know if your partner is frustrated, bold, angry, or bored. It will be apparent in the way she carries her tail, in how she cocks an ear, and in the way she walks. You finally will begin approaching the level of observation your horse has for you. And, this instinctive knowledge you have for each other will serve you both well in the future.

CHAPTER 15

HANG TEN

Throughout My Horse, My Partner training, you have combined desensitization activities with traditional groundwork, and each activity has raised the bar in some way. You have progressed in an orderly fashion and introduced concepts and objects to your partner in a manner and in a time frame that he understands. You have taken time to really get to know your partner during this process and have taken your relationship to an entirely new level. Now you and your equine friend are ready for a final desensitization exercise.

Not too long ago I was at a horse clinic where I heard another clinician speak against desensitization. "It just doesn't work," he said. "All that stuff flapping around and hanging all over them just scares them and they are never right after that."

In a sense, he is correct. Many people become so excited about the concept of imprinting and desensitization that they wave a few plastic bags in their horse's face and then throw everything in the barn on top of the horse. The horse then, of course, is so overwhelmed that he panics. The difference here is that you have worked slowly and for many months to bring your partner toward increasing levels of trust, confidence, and respect. You have learned to recognize signs of acceptance and unease, and have been careful throughout the process not to overload his mind with ideas he is not ready to accept. All of that has now paid off.

Valentino is responsive as I back him through cones. His attire includes a pom-pom between his ears, two sets of bells, a feed sack folded underneath the ladder reins, and several plastic bags.

First, you have a horse who trusts you. Even when he is hesitant to accept a new object, he does so because he knows you would not ask him to do anything that would hurt him. You also have an equine friend who cares about you as much as he is capable of caring about any human. He cares because you have shown him great consideration, because you have made efforts to relate to him on his terms, and because you have shown him that *you* care.

Now, because you both are ready, it is time to complete the desensitization process.

HANG TEN, ONE AT A TIME

For this activity you will need the ladder reins, and the surcingle or the saddle you used for the earlier hanging activity. Go back to your "safe place" (the round pen or the paddock you have been working in) and bring with you your entire toolkit. Also bring your partner, haltered and tacked.

Begin by introducing the pom-pom and reaccustom his mind and body to it. When he tells you with his lowered head and his licking and chewing that he has accepted it, place it as you did in Chapter Five under his halter and between his ears.

Next find a piece of plastic or other object your friend has shown a preference for. Reintroduce it to your horse just as you did the pom-pom. Then tuck it under a corner of the saddle or surcingle, or wrap it up in a bit clip and hook it to the ladder reins.

Then stand back to observe your friend as he processes the two objects. It is fairly easy for a horse to focus on one object, but two can sometimes be confusing. Give him all the time he needs; most horses will not need much at all.

When he's accepted wearing the pom-pom and the other object, begin adding, one at a time, items such as towels, plastic, stuffed animals, aluminum cans in a bag, bells, and other previously introduced objects. Each time after you add an object, stand back to let him process this new addition. You might be able to add one new item an hour, a day, or a week. You are a team, and can only go as fast or slow as you can. Your work or family commitments might slow you down one week, and your partner's hesitancy about things that are purple might slow you down the next. Remember to be as patient with your partner as he is with you.

As you hook and clip items to the saddle or surcingle, be sure to keep comfort and safety in mind. Nothing should bang or bump your horse. Nothing should hang lower than knee level. Nothing should be hung that could injure your friend in any way. If your horse shows discomfort or unease with a specific object, move it to a different spot, or replace it with another. If you give your partner time to process each new object after it is hung, you will be able to quickly identify anything that makes your friend uncomfortable—and just as quickly be able to change it.

PASTURE TIME

Once your partner is fully loaded with eight to ten objects, let him hang out in the round pen or paddock for a while. You can throw him a flake of hay, but otherwise leave him alone to get used to feeling and hearing the new objects on his body.

When your horse tells you he has accepted this turn of events, if he has not already done so, encourage him to move at a walk around his small enclosure. Just waving your hand at him and saying "walk on" will probably be enough at this point. Keep him moving for a few minutes, to become comfortable with the idea of moving so he does

Bad Behavior

Keep in mind that biting, kicking, and striking are often signs of distress. If your partner is exhibiting these behaviors, you may have missed earlier warning signs such as a swishing tail, swinging head, or pinned ears. These warning signs can mean you are going faster than your horse is comfortable with. Be sure to keep a close eye on your friend as you work to specify the exact source of the trouble, and then backtrack to a level that is more comfortable. Remember that repetition makes the extraordinary routine.

not become startled when you lead him out of the enclosure. Then lead him out to his pasture (still dressed up) or wherever he usually spends his day. Be cautious going through gates, as the objects hanging from your friend add quite a bit of width. You want to be sure you do not catch a bag or pom-pom on a hinge or latch.

If your partner can spend all afternoon in the pasture, let him. The more time he can spend with the various objects blowing gently in the breeze, the better. Take a book or some music and watch from a corner. Or take the opportunity to check the fence and bring a hammer and some nails with you as you do your inspection. Do a little weed eating or bush hogging. In each situation you are able to supervise your horse from a distance. If he were to become alarmed or somehow get into trouble, you are but a minute away.

When Valentino was at this level in his training, I sent him out to a small pasture to hang with a few of his friends, Nacho being one of them. Valentino could have cared less about all the stuff hanging from him. But Nacho was enthralled. He came trotting up to Valentino and immediately began pulling at each of the objects. Valentino very nicely asked Nacho to leave him alone by turning his rump toward him and by briefly lifting his head and pinning his ears at Nacho between bites of grass. When Nacho did not listen, Valentino became a little more aggressive, and turned his head to bare his teeth at Nacho. Finally, Valentino kicked out with a hind leg. I realized that Nacho was having too much fun to pay attention, so instead of removing Valentino from the pasture, I removed Nacho. Nacho got to spend a few hours in a paddock with a cute little mare, and Valentino became fully accustomed to the trappings of desensitization.

LEADING

Leading your horse around the farm while he is carrying everything should not be a big deal to you, or to him. But because your partner now looks as if he just flew in from Mars to other horses and to any farm dogs you might have roaming around, it might be a really big deal. For that reason, be sure to let others who are spending time with their own equine friends know what your partner will be wearing, and that he may also be making an assortment of rustling and jingling sounds. And if they show the least bit of aggression, farm dogs should be removed from sight of your partner.

Even though your horse is now comfortable with his new wardrobe in the pasture, he may still welcome your presence and feel safer with you, his dominant partner, by his side. But on another level, he may not be fully comfortable with you leading him. This is because he has freedom over his actions and movements in the pasture, but when being led, the halter and lead restrict him. Your friend also may not have done much turning in the pasture. When you turn your partner in a tight circle, or when you reverse direction, he will see out of the corner of his eye a different view of all that he is carrying. The new view may startle him, or he may not react at all.

The noise of your partner's getup may also make him uncomfortable. When you are leading him, if a gust of wind blows up to send everything crackling, banging, and rustling, he may not perceive it as the same thing that happened when he was grazing in his pasture. That's why it is important to practice, practice, practice, over and over in many different locations. Lead your horse around the farm and set up several patterns for the two of you to do together so he becomes thoroughly used to the weight, noise, and movement of the excess baggage he is carrying around, no matter what you ask him to do.

Some horses, like Lady, are instinctively comfortable with their odd new clothes. Lady's mission in life is to eat every single blade of grass that she can. Everything else is, in her mind, beside the point and not worth getting excited about. Lady very pleasantly accepts new things, but to her, nothing is more interesting than eating. With some herd groups she has been a leader, but she prefers to be in the middle of the pack and let others make the decisions. Lady is, by nature, hungry.

Other horses, like Nomo, always remain somewhat cautious. Nomo's self-appointed job in life is to take care of others. In her herd she is the first to lift her head when an unusual smell or sound comes across her radar. With a rider on her back she is hesitant about anything new. She doesn't whirl around to run, but her approach is cautious until she has determined what the new object is and decided it is safe. She is, by nature, protective.

These two mares are very different, yet they are both very good therapeutic riding horses. Each has gone through My Horse, My Partner training and each has accepted different items on different timelines. I know I can go out at any time and load Lady up with toolkit items and she will not bat an eye. Nomo needs a short reintroduction to every item each time she sees it.

You know by now exactly who your partner is. He may be more like Lady, and you can just load him up and go. Or he may be more like Nomo, wanting the reassurance of seeing each item one more time before he agrees to let it be hooked to him. He may lead perfectly through an intricate pattern while all dressed up, or he may have to work hard to focus on the task at hand with all the distraction swirling around him.

And that, ultimately, is the big benefit of this activity: creating close and continual distraction, so your partner can learn to focus on you, and on the direction you give him. It's learning to expect—and prepare for—the unexpected. It's learning to give his best with the swirl of horse-show activity around him, or the excitement of more than a hundred horses on a trail ride. And in an emergency, focus versus panic can mean the difference between life and death, and between a minor injury and broken limbs.

LONGEING

Longeing adds increased speed and movement. When you longed your friend with one object, you were careful that the item did not bang or bump your friend. Today, with ten or so objects, you need to

Valentino's raised head shows that he is uncertain about picking up the trot. Lots of praise with a firm voice eventually relaxed him enough canter comfortably.

be very certain of the placement of each. If you have to stop to move or readjust an item, by all means stop and readjust.

Always be sure your horse is comfortable and confident, first at the walk and then at the trot, before asking for a canter or lope. Remember that the noise and movement of the objects vary from gait to gait. So, while your equine partner may have categorized this process at the walk and the trot as safe, the canter—with its new movement of objects—will be perceived by your partner as completely different from other gaits.

The movement and noise of higher speeds may cause your partner some initial concern. Watch his head, neck, ears, eyes, and tail. If the head and neck are elevated, the eyes wide and the tail swishing, something is bothering him. Drop back to a walk. Then, when he is showing you he is relaxed, ask for an increase in speed, but only maintain it for a few strides. Be sure to give your horse effusive praise for responding correctly. Slowly, as he relaxes over time, you can extend the number of strides in the faster gait.

You can also remove some of the noisier or larger objects. Go back to two items, then three. Gradually add objects back in until you find the one that causes concern. Also check the placement of the remaining objects. The problem might be as simple as a bag that is hitting an elbow.

If your partner panics, calmly use the "whoa" hand and voice signals, then remove a few of the objects. Remember that your partner will look to you for guidance. If you have listened to your horse, you know how much or little he is able to handle and will have given him only what he is able to process. Keep in mind that in addition to desensitization, this is about focus and it may be a tough assignment for your partner. Don't expect miracles. If your partner gets it right off the bat, fabulous! If he is relaxed and correctly responds to all your cues, it is a real achievement for you both. But if it takes a few weeks (or longer), be patient.

If your horse is having trouble with this activity, or with anything you ask him to do, remember to look to yourself. You and your friend are a team. Are you inadvertently or subconsciously telling your partner that he should be nervous about this latest activity? Are you projecting a lack of confidence that he is picking up on? Are you telling him with your tense body, strained voice, and tight facial muscles that there is something to fear? All of those things must be taken into consideration.

It is okay if you discover that you need more practice than your horse does. It happens all the time. You have been patient with your partner, and he will be patient with you. If this is the case, think back to where you lost your level of comfort. Then go back to that activity, and work up again slowly from there. Be sure not to rush yourself or your horse; he needs you to feel fully comfortable with every activity.

LONG LINING

There are two major differences between regular long lining and long lining with toolkit items attached to your partner. The first is that the lines may rub across a piece of plastic, a towel, or a pom-pom. This will create an unexpected noise, and also may interfere with the angle or positioning of the line, which affects communication between you and your horse. The second is the increased difficulty in raising the lines over the pile of stuff on your equine friend's rump. Both take a little practice to perfect.

Also remember that when changing tracks, your partner is bending in ways he did not during the longeing process. When you led him through patterns, you hopefully included a number of turns. The difference between that scenario and this one is that when you were leading your friend, you were close to him. He had the comfort and security of knowing that you were right there to take care of any trouble that cropped up.

When you are long lining, you are standing much farther away from your horse. He then has to take on much more responsibility for his own safety, which may or may not be threatened by the sound, movement, and weight of the objects he is carrying. For reassurance, he will look to you and what your body posture is telling him.

Realize that if your friend normally has difficulty with an activity, that he will most likely do less well in these circumstances than he normally does, so do not expect the performance level to be the same at first. In the best of circumstances, Nacho has terrible difficulty navigating over poles. When he is carrying plastic bags, pots and pans, pom-poms, and stuffed animals, it is distracting for him. In Nacho's mind, he is carrying a walking toy chest, and the temptation is great. That means if we are long lining over a pole, most of his mind is on the potential toys that are so close at hand, and only a little part is left to process everything else involved in getting himself safely over a pole.

GROUND DRIVING

The final step in this activity is to move from long lining to ground driving. And again, there are a few areas to watch out for.

If you have placed items on your horse's rump, be sure the objects do not break the line of the reins so much that you lose communication with him. Normally, your partner can also "feel" the lines going across his rump. But now, depending on where you have placed different items, his rump may be completely covered in plastic or feed sacks. It is not necessarily a bad thing, but you do have to be aware that your friend may no longer be able to feel a shake of the rein on his hindquarters. If you use this method to help him move forward, you will need to rely on your voice as a means of communication.

Also, as you know, vocal communication is very important in driving, but if the objects hanging from your equine friend are making a lot of noise, he will not be able to hear you when you speak to him. In this case, you might think about replacing the noisier items with quieter ones.

Visually, your horse's very limited view of you in the driving position is probably blocked completely by the extra width of bags and other objects along his sides. So, where he could catch glimpses of you before when negotiating turns, that visual is now not available.

When you are ready to set up a pattern to drive through, keep in mind that trust and confidence really have to come to the forefront. As your partner negotiates over and through obstacles, he has to do so with only the reins and your voice to guide him. He can't see you. He may have difficulty hearing you, and because there is a bunch of "stuff" in the way, the pull of the reins is going to feel unusual. These are extreme circumstances for sure, but you may be surprised at how well you both do.

Additionally, what confidence you project to your horse has to come through your strong and relaxed voice, the firm set of directions given by your hands, and that instinctive "feel" discussed earlier. Rest assured, if you are nervous, your partner knows it, just as you can tell if he is nervous.

RESULTS!

Remember in Chapter One, I mentioned standing in the center of Middle Tennessee State University's Tennessee Miller Coliseum about to longe Valentino with all his trappings? Valentino had taken twelve months of regular and consistent sessions to get to this point. Since then, he has begun teaching children with disabilities to ride and love horses, has served as a lesson horse for some of the Saddle Up! instructors to better their skills, and just recently was used as a pattern horse for prospective North American Riding for the Handicapped Association (NARHA) instructors to become certified. Valentino is still just four years old. But it doesn't end there. In addition to being featured in a number of newscasts and television shows, just before *My Horse, My Partner* is published, Valentino will serve as one of ten practice horses for Special Olympic riders who will be representing the United States at the 2007 World Summer Games in Shanghai, China.

This little abandoned rescue horse has come a long, long way. I say this not to brag about him, although I am extraordinarily proud, but to reinforce the fact that if Valentino can do this, he can do just about anything. More importantly, once you have given your horse all the tools he needs, he can do just about anything, too. And so can you.

There is just one big step left to accomplish, so let's get to it.

HITCH 'EM UP

The final My Horse, My Partner activity is learning to pull a travois, a rudimentary sled used for centuries by many Native American tribes to haul belongings, and by countless equine enthusiasts to teach a horse to pull. A travois is made of two poles (one for each side of the horse) and held together by a pole across the ends. Pulling a heavy travois, or one loaded with noisy or visual items, is the ultimate test in trust, respect, and confidence.

EQUIPMENT

BUILDING A TRAVOIS

Even for those of you who are not handy with a hammer, a travois is very easy to build. In fact, you don't even need a hammer. What you do need are two approximately four-inch by four-inch square posts, or a rounded equivalent. You can use a smaller post or pole, but 4x4s are very stable and are the perfect weight for this activity. The poles should be six to eight feet in length—or a little shorter if your partner is a pony. The third "pole" should be a 2x4 about four feet long. The two long poles will become the shafts (or sides) of the travois, and the shorter one will be the crossbar that holds everything together. You can go to your local home improvement store to get the posts, or you might have something usable out behind the barn.

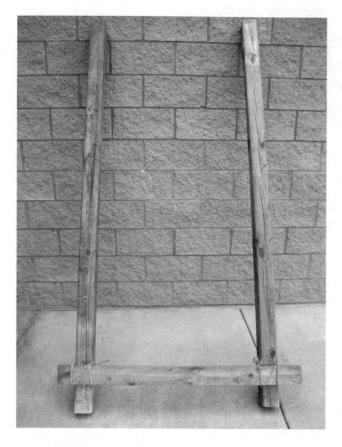

A sturdy travois is easy to make.

To keep the travois free of metal, baling twine makes great lashing.

Before you put the travois together, check the posts or poles thoroughly to be sure there are no splintered areas, and no major cracks in the wood. You certainly do not want the pole to break into two pieces the first time you begin to drive, nor do you want any possibility of a splinter coming near you or your partner.

Also make sure the travois is wide enough for your equine friend. To check the fit, lay the two poles side by side, and then lead your horse between them. Adjust the width so there are several inches on either side of the widest point of your partner's barrel or rump. Because most horses are wider at the barrel and rump than they are at their feet, you may have to pick up one end of the pole and raise it to see if there is enough clearance.

When you have the width accurately calculated, lead your partner straight through the poles without disturbing them, and put her in a round pen or a pasture. You won't need her for a few minutes so she might as well be comfortable. Then go back to the travois and place the shorter pole on top of and across the two longer poles about six inches from one end. The shorter pole should extend beyond the width of the longer poles four to ten inches on either side.

There are several ways to join the poles together, including long nails or screws, or drilling a hole and using a metal connector through the hole. But I prefer the simple method of lashing the poles together with baling twine or clothesline rope. First, it's easy. I am not all that mechanically minded, but I can tie poles together. Second, it is quick and inexpensive. Third, it is easily adjustable. If you lash too narrow or too wide, it is more easily

fixed than pulling out a nail or a screw, or drilling another hole. And fourth (and most important) I like the idea that if the travois came apart for some reason, there are no nails or other metal parts that could injure my equine partner or me.

If you are handy with tools, you can also add wheels to your travois. The best place to add them is to the underside at the ends of the long poles, below the crossbar. An assortment of wheels can be found at home improvement or farm supply stores, but the wider the tire tread the better. Also, wheels that swivel, such as those found on an office supply cart, work best, as do smaller wheels that do not lift the end of the travois too far off the ground.

This basic travois plan can be modified in many ways, and with a little experimentation, you will find exactly the right fit for you.

This homemade harness includes Nacho's regular bridle, longe lines for reins, a longeing surcingle, and two sidereins for the breastplate. The travois is attached to the harness by an 18-inch length of sturdy chain that is wrapped around the side pole and attached to the longeing surcingle with an S hook.

THE HARNESS

Before you can actually hook your horse to the travois, you will need a harness of some sort. If you have a regular harness, by all means use it. If not, don't worry. You already have most, if not all, of the equipment needed to rig up a makeshift harness.

Begin with your surcingle. In addition, you will need some sort of a breastplate. A martingale or breastplate that hooks to the front of a saddle works well for this purpose. An English stirrup leather, one side rein, a Western cinch, or a short lead rope can also be modified to work. Whatever you use, it has to connect to one side of the surcingle, pass across the front of your partner's chest, and then connect to the other side of the surcingle. This gives your partner something to pull against.

THE BRIDLE

A bridle and reins are also necessary. For reins you can use driving reins, a set of long lines, or two longe lines.

Blinkers can be also be found on some harness bridles, and if you are using a harness that has them, remove them if at all possible. This activity works best if a horse has a larger view than blinkers provide. If the blinkers can't be removed, substitute your regular bridle and snaffle bit for the ones that belong with the harness.

ALTERNATIVES

A saddle and breastplate can work instead of a harness or a surcingle, but remove the stirrups first, as they can get in the way of the travois's side poles. But no matter what equipment you use, ensure that each piece of equipment is in good working condition. Equipment should also be adjusted so that it does not poke or prod your equine friend in any way.

HOOKING UP

One last step is needed before you can begin driving. There has to be something on the harness to hook the travois to. The front end of the travois should be fastened to something near the front of the saddle, or to the surcingle, so it lies midway between your partner's withers and elbow. This can be accomplished in several ways. Medium-weight rope, chains, or leather straps of 18 to 24 inches can be wrapped around the front of each long pole, then hooked to a bit clip attached to the saddle or surcingle. To prevent the chain or strap from slipping off the front of the pole, you can wrap duct tape tightly or use more baling twine between the chain and the end of the pole to create a bulge that the chain cannot slip over.

Another option is to place a large, blunt-edged hook on the bottom of the pole near where the chain or strap will lie, with the open end of the hook facing your partner's tail. The placement of the hook on the underside of the long pole is relatively safe and is not likely to injure your equine friend in any way. Then you can loop the chain through the hook.

Note that traditional carts and buggies have shafts or side poles that are much longer than those on a travois, often reaching to the front of the horse's chest and beyond. The danger with a travois lies in the fact that you are standing on the ground, versus sitting higher up in a wheeled vehicle. Your lower presence, and the increased angle from bit to withers to your hand, increases the possibility that your reins will get hooked around the shafts. To prevent that, we use shorter poles. Be sure, too, that your reins are attached to the highest point possible near your horse's withers. This further reduces the possibility of a rein catching on a side pole.

Nacho stands patiently, ready for his next cue. Note that I am standing far enough behind the travois that I will not inadvertently trip over it.

In driving, your voice is one of a very few aids you can use. Here, Nacho's ears indicate he is listening to me.

HITCHING UP

If your partner has never before pulled anything, enlist the aid of a helper. Lay the travois flat on the ground and let your equine friend inspect it. If you and your helper raise the travois by lifting the front ends evenly, this gives your partner a new view.

The fact that the travois is simply wood and rope helps most horses accept it very quickly. If your friend shows any concern, move the travois to her paddock or round pen, prop it up on a fence and let your partner have all the time with it that she needs.

When the introduction process is complete, bring your friend to a large, enclosed area, such as a riding ring or large paddock, with no other horses present. Position the travois in such a way that when you and your horse begin to drive, you can start on a long, straight path, rather than immediately having to navigate a corner. Harness your friend and position her so her rear legs are just in front of the travois. Then back her a few steps until the front of the travois is near her girth area. Once you are sure she is relaxed, you and your helper can each take a side and quickly fasten the long poles of the travois to the saddle or surcingle.

THE FIRST DRIVE

If your horse is pulling for the first time, it is best if you stay by her head and control her with a halter and lead, or bit clips attached to the bit rings, while your helper stands well behind the crossbar of the travois in the driver position. Your partner trusts you, and having you by her side will help her learn to pull. Although the travois probably weighs less than one hundred pounds, it is weighty enough that a horse who has never pulled before may become confused. Your presence at her head will reassure her that she is doing well. And, while the driver is not actively driving, having someone in that position will acquaint your partner with seeing someone behind the travois.

At first just walk a straight line for thirty or forty feet and stop. Be sure to praise your partner for a job well done. Then plan your first turn. The combined length of horse, travois, and driver is now well over twelve feet. And because horses who are hitched to anything are confined by shafts, it is nearly impossible for them to bend. You will not be able to turn nearly as sharply as you have in the past, so plan big, slow, sweeping turns.

As you begin the turn, remember that this is the first time your partner will be able to see a corner of the travois. As she turns to the right, the back of the travois will swing slightly to the left. She may also feel unaccustomed pressure from the front of the right shaft, or pole. Your voice and relaxed but firm manner will help her get used to these new sights and feelings.

The first time I hooked Nacho to a travois, he was fine until we attempted a turn. When he glimpsed the travois out of the corner of his eye, he thought that was pretty cool and slowly turned around to get a better look at it. Of course, the travois turned with him. When Nacho figured out that he couldn't get closer to the travois by going to the right, he simply turned the other direction. If he couldn't turn right to get at it, then maybe he needed to turn left. When Nacho realized that strategy wouldn't work either, he settled in to the task at hand: pulling. I could tell by Nacho's loose lips, relaxed skin, lowered head, and calm ears that he was not upset or frightened. He just had discovered a great new toy and wanted to check it out. Even though Nacho had been a driving horse in an Amish or Mennonite community before he came to Saddle Up!, the feel of the travois was different to him, and he thought it was fun.

Before we hitched him to it, Nacho had the opportunity to check out the travois. And in typical Nacho fashion he nuzzled every inch of it with his lips. But in his compartmentalized brain, the object Nacho nuzzled while it was lying flat on the ground was not the same object that was now attached to him. He wanted to explore this "new" object in the way he explores best, with his lips. It took some convincing with firm voice and body posture that it would be just as fun for him to move forward. Eventually, he agreed.

When practicing straight lines and wide turns, watch your partner closely for signs of distress or acceptance. If your horse is uncomfortable, just stop and talk to her until she shows you she is more relaxed. It may be that all you get done the first few sessions is to hook up, walk a few steps, and unhook. Look to your horse. She will tell you how quickly she wants to proceed. When your equine friend is at least somewhat comfortable with the travois and with pulling, you can switch places with your helper. When you make the switch, your helper will become a passive leader, in position only for safety and emotional support. You, as the driver, will actively take control.

First get your bearings. Be sure you are standing well behind the travois, or you will trip over it. When you ask your partner to walk on, she may hesitate, so keep your voice pleasant, but firm. Your partner will draw strength from the solid tone of your voice. Earlier, when you stood by your horse's head, your presence reassured her that all was well. Now, with you behind her, she may not be as confident—so be patient.

Begin with simple walk/whoa and whoa/walk transitions, and those big, wide turns. Trotting is not necessary at this point; just concentrate on perfecting the basics until you each are comfortable. And that shouldn't take too long, as your earlier driving activities should transfer well to the travois. All the items you hung from your partner should have accustomed her to things she cannot get away from, like the travois. The two new areas here are the sight of the travois behind her, and the feel of it as she pulls.

I've done travois work with horses as young as eighteen months. Not right off the bat, of course. Each youngster had gone through all of the previous activities first. But the one thing that confuses horses of every age at first is the weight of the travois. Unless a horse has previously been driven or pulled a cart, it takes them some time to understand what to do.

As you and your partner practice, your helper can gradually move away. Eventually, he or she can move to a corner of your driving area to be available in case assistance is needed.

TROTTING

If you read your horse closely, you will know when it is time to attempt a trot with the travois. Complete acceptance of the entire basic process is needed first. That will not come overnight, so be sure to give your partner enough time to feel fully comfortable with the travois at the walk, and on turns, before asking for a trot.

When you do ask for the first time, bring your helper back in to stand at your partner's head. The travois will feel different to your friend as she moves into this new gait, and your helper can reassure her, if needed.

Turns at the trot can be extremely awkward, so unless you are fairly athletic yourself, keep your travois trots confined to the straightaway.

THE PULL OF PATTERNS

When your horse is pulling a travois and the two of you are negotiating a pattern, you have to work as a team. You each have to read every possible signal the other is sending and respond appropriately. That is why it is especially important that you send strong, consistent cues to your partner. If your signals are the least bit inconsistent, she will become easily confused . . . and so will you!

You will, however, have to make a few changes to the patterns you have been doing to accommodate the travois. First of all, do not attempt to go over any poles (flat or raised), or to step over anything on the ground such as a tarp or plywood. Also do not go over anything raised, like a bridge, or through a water hazard. The wheels or ground edge of the travois could catch on any of these items and jar your partner to a sudden halt. Traveling over regular ground is enough of a challenge.

While you may be extremely proud of the tight figure eights and serpentines you and your partner can perform at the trot or canter when long lining, the cones or markers you weave through will have to be spaced farther apart when pulling a travois. Obviously, the extra length of the rig, and the shafts that prevent your horse from bending, contribute to this change. Remember, too, the opposite swing of the travois. When making a left turn, the travois will swing to the right, so it will take extra skill to guide your partner through these markers without hitting them, or knocking them over. And even if your partner willingly responds to a cue for a sharp turn, know that the ends of the poles could dig into her shoulder, so take care to keep the turns wide.

LOADING UP

You have probably guessed by now that the final step in this activity is to combine the travois, driving, and communication with desensi-

tization and items from your toolkit. And not only can you load your horse up with toolkit objects, you can load up the travois.

Traditionally, the back half of a travois was very long and had an animal skin stretched between the side poles. Native Americans would then load their belongings, and sometimes even their children, onto the skin for their long journey. Our travois is not long enough to stretch anything between the poles, but you can tie plastic bags filled with aluminum cans, feed bags, stuffed ani-

Nacho remains focused as he pulls a travois through a pattern. Attached to the travois are two plastic bags filled with crushed (and noisy) aluminum cans.

mals, or even a string of bells to the side poles and to the crossbar.

As previously, your horse should have the opportunity to inspect each object before it is placed on the travois. Ideally, this should happen before she is hitched so that she does not feel too confined. And, as before, begin with just one object.

Where you position an item is also critical. If you hang an object from the shafts, be sure that it does not bump your partner's legs on straight lines or during turns. A bag of aluminum cans, for example, would be better positioned on top of your partner, or low on the shaft, near or on the crossbar. On the other hand, a pom-pom might rustle, but it is incapable of banging.

When your horse is comfortable with pulling the first object, introduce the next and add it to the travois. Never add a new object before your equine friend is comfortable with pulling the earlier object (or objects). If after much time and patience you get the feeling your partner is actively resisting a specific item, remove it, set it aside, and move on to another. You can always go back and reintroduce it later.

This entire process clearly takes time. But when you remember that you are developing a partnership with your equine friend that will last a lifetime, it is definitely time well spent.

RESULTS!

With both horse and human confident in this final step, each of you should have developed an incredible level of trust and confidence in, and respect for, each other. Hopefully you have developed a new and deeper understanding not only of your equine partner, but also of yourself. These activities are designed as much for you, the human partner, as they are for the horses we all love so much.

You have taken the time to learn the language of your equine friend, and through that, you have grown by leaps and bounds as a horseman or horsewoman. Now it is time to learn how to share bits and pieces of your knowledge with other horses, and with other people.

**Through time and practice, you can become an expert at understanding
every nuance of your individual equine friend.**

PUTTING IT ALL TOGETHER 17

Depending on your existing skill level and on the age, temperament, and training of your partner when you began, it may have taken you several weeks to get to this point. Or it may have taken months, or even years. Every horse/human team is different, and each partnership has individual challenges to overcome. But let's see what you have learned.

PATIENCE

Most likely, you found patience you didn't know you had. With some horses, I spend weeks just tossing a pom-pom against their sides. Inside, I get so frustrated that sometimes I want to jump up and down and wave my arms and scream. That, of course, wouldn't get us anywhere . . . but I've thought it many times all the same.

I have found that just when I am ready to give up, just when I think my equine friend will never grasp a particular concept, it all falls together. I've often been ready to give up when I tell myself "just five more minutes," or "just one more session," or "until the end of the week." Invariably, that "extra" time is when my partner finally understands whatever activity we are working on. You have possibly had those same thoughts and experiences.

You have perhaps also experienced the uncanny perception of your equine friend. If you are tense or upset, no matter how you try to hide it, your horse still knows. So you have learned to relax and tune out the rest of the world while you and your equine friend move forward. You also have come to understand that acceptance of any activity will hap-

Your new and confident leading skills will help you establish connections with any horse at any time, and for both short and long term relationships.

pen in his time frame, not yours. All of that takes a great deal of patience.

DETERMINATION

You never would have accomplished all you have with your partner if you were not determined. Whether you realize it or not, you have learned to consider each difficulty you encounter with your equine friend as a personal challenge. I am sure that at some point you have asked yourself the following questions: What can I do to make this concept clearer? What signal is my partner sending me that I am missing? What approach have I not taken? What conflicting cues am I sending to my horse that makes this difficult for him? What part do I need to go back and repeat? In short, you were determined to succeed—and you did!

I believe my equine partners recognize a determined mindset and take confidence from it. Sometimes you have to go in with the attitude that, "We are going to get this done. It might take three months, but together, we *are* going to do this." You learned to take your many successes in small amounts, and you carried on. That's determination.

COMMITMENT

By now you fully realize that developing your talents—and those of your equine partner—takes commitment. Nothing could have been achieved unless you were committed to your goal. This includes setting aside time.

As you have found, you do not have to spend hours a day working as a team with your partner to see benefits from My Horse, My Partner activities. Those of you who spent five or six hours a week probably progressed faster than those who spent two hours a week. I say "probably" because much depends on you and your partner. I can take an older, quiet, retired show pony, and spending an hour every day, we might complete everything in five or six weeks. Then again, I could spend an hour every day with a younger horse who was not handled much as a baby and who has never been off the farm, and it might take us a year and a half . . . or longer.

But whatever the time frame, you completed a huge project bit by bit, and eventually, you finished every part of it. You have definitely proven that you take commitment seriously.

CONFIDENCE

Sometimes you get so close to something that you can't see the forest for the trees. I am willing to bet that even though you may not realize it, your friends will tell you that you have become a more confident person as a result of My Horse, My Partner activities. My Horse, My Partner is as much a program for the human as it is for the horse, although your equine friend is likely more confident as well.

I began writing this book about the same time Lucky came to Saddle Up! Always the most passive horse in his group, Lucky has lately been standing up to his herd. Although he is only about halfway through the activities, Lucky has recently demonstrated new confidence in himself. A few days ago, several Saddle Up! volunteers and I witnessed Lucky "herding" his small group, which included Nelson and Valentino, around a paddock. He busily pushed them into corners, made them circle first one direction and then the next at a gallop, and generally ignored the pinned ears and kicks the others sent his way. This, for Lucky, was a huge breakthrough. Months before, he would have stayed in the corner while the others played. Now he is not only instigating play, he is controlling it. Lucky has also been more confident under saddle and is accepting new things more quickly. I can't wait to see what Lucky will become by the time he finishes the rest of the activities.

TRUST

Through confidence, you have developed trust. You now know your horse so well and are so confident of his specific abilities that you trust him to take care of you. You trust that he will be a strong, steady mount, that he will stop if danger presents itself, that he will listen to you, and that he will try his best to do what you ask.

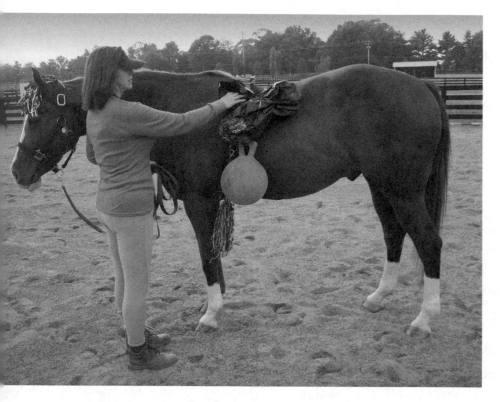

Trust is an earned privilege between humans. This concept is even truer when you are dealing with horses. Through the activities you have done together, your equine partner honors your trust in him. He also expects you to honor the trust he has placed in you. You have worked very hard to earn this status with your friend, so please be very careful that you do not do anything in the future to lose it. Consistent and fair behavior from you, along with continued attempts to understand what your friend is telling you, will solidify your partner's trust for years to come.

Even though Nelson has a laid-back attitude, he has a very intelligent and sharp mind. It takes a while, though, to get past the exterior to learn all of the wonderful, hidden qualities your equine partner has.

FRIENDSHIP

When I was fourteen, my Appaloosa mare, Snoqualmie, was pregnant with her colt, Ben. On the day I expected her to give birth, I arrived in the barn quietly and early, only to find Snoqualmie panicked at the sudden changes within her body. Her eyes were wild as she frantically paced up and down her stall. But the instant she saw me, Snoqualmie quieted. Her eyes and body relaxed, she gave a huge, calming sigh, and the rest of the birth went very peacefully. I was struck at the time, and even more so as the years have passed, that the mere sight of me would make her feel more secure. Snoqualmie was very confident in her trust of me; as long as I was there, everything would be just fine.

Years later, we were separated for a time when I moved out of state. When I finally had her trailered to my new home, Snoqualmie walked into the barn with a great deal of hesitation. But when she saw me she gave a huge whinny and literally pulled her handler down the aisle until she could place her face against my chest. Once again, she sighed.

And isn't that how we feel about our human friends? When we become separated, we are happy when we are reunited with them. In times of need and stress, we automatically turn to our friends. And because we know them so well, we know whether to provide laughter, moral support, or action. You and your equine partner now have that special bond of friendship. Each of you instinctively knows what the other needs and will do your best to provide it. Additionally, you truly enjoy each other's company. That's friendship.

PRIDE

I hope you are proud of yourself, of your equine partner, and of your accomplishments together. You each have come a long very way in your understanding of each other. Through your shared activities, you have become a far better horse person, and your equine friend has become a far better companion.

Pride in a job well done is necessary for both humans and horses. It builds positive self-esteem and through that, confidence and trust. As you have probably noticed, these traits are all intertwined and circle back around to each other frequently. It is difficult to have one without the others.

In addition to the time I spend in the equestrian world, I speak to groups and businesses across the country on motivation and success. Unfortunately, through those speaking presentations, I have found two of the toughest things for most of us to do are to show pride in ourselves, and to acknowledge our own accomplishments. For most of us, it is very difficult to give ourselves a pat on the back. In this case, I hope you allow yourself to enjoy your achievements! It is not only important to praise your equine partner when he does well, it is important for you to be proud and recognize your accomplishments.

Even if you and your partner did not fully complete all the My Horse, My Partner activities, know that every activity you completed is a mini-success. Every step accomplished is a step toward new understanding of your partner, and of horses in general.

Take time to applaud yourself, because you deserve the praise. And be proud of yourself and your partner, for you have reached a level of skill and perception that few other horse/human partners achieve.

In case you have forgotten how far you have actually come, here are a few reminders of your specific accomplishments. In no particular order, you learned:

1. to organize a toolkit; to differentiate from a horse's perspective between objects that have color, sound, and movement; how to discover your horse's likes and dislikes, including her preferences in music and color; and why it is important to cater to your partner's preferences.

2. about new pieces of tack, such as ladder reins and bit clips; the correct way to fit a halter; how to correctly fit a saddle and a surcingle; and correct bridle fitting.

3. to get to know your equine friend's body, including how to find the "tickle" spots; and to assess your partner's health by looking at her body.

4. to go at your partner's pace rather than your own; how to move your equine friend to higher levels with zero stress; to identify signs of trust and decipher your equine friend's moods and peculiarities; signs of acceptance and distress; to be patient; and how to recognize and use your own intuition.

5. safe and unsafe areas in working around your horse; to lead safely; to teach your friend to stop, no matter what; how and when to use hand signals; consideration for other horses and riders; why you are your partner's safety net; and safety procedures when driving.

6. proper methods of discipline; the correct use of a lead chain; why there are no "quick fixes;" cures for biting; how to focus your horse in new locations; and corrections for bad leading habits.

7. how to relate to your partner on her level; how horses see the world; typical and atypical behaviors for your horse; understanding the compartmentalization of your partner's brain; how to think like a horse; how horses learn; why familiarity is everything and repetition is key; to find the best timeline for you and your partner; how to watch your horse without being watched; and how to work with your friend's strengths and weaknesses.

8. the importance of your facial expressions, body posture, and voice cues; and how tone of voice affects response.

9. to desensitize gently; the importance of working on both the left and right; why having good rhythm is critical; how horses interpret your movements; why hanging objects from your partner develops trust; how to hang multiple objects; to work with your partner with objects that move and make noise; how to quickly re-introduce old objects; why consistency is important; how to work as a team with your partner; and that success means practicing over and over again.

10. the importance of voice commands and tone of voice; why praise is necessary.

11. how sensitive a horse's ears can be, how to overcome that sensitivity, and to handle a horse's ears carefully.

12. to assess your partner's leading skills; to lead at the trot, in a circle and in a serpentine; how to lead in patterns; to lead without a halter; and backing strategies.

13. how to play with a horse; to teach your partner to differentiate between work and play; to recognize your friend's signs of frustration; how playing with your partner strengthens your relationship; how to establish rules; to find ideas for games, to assess toys for safety; and how play helps with traditional training methods.

14. the difference between free longeing and using a longe line, and the benefits of each; plus longeing techniques, troubleshooting, and safety; how to long line and drive your partner, and how these activities develop confidence and communication.

15. what horses hear that humans do not; how to use sound-effect CDs; how to introduce various noises without frightening your friend; and how sounds build confidence and stimulate your equine partner's brain.

16. to teach your horse to pull; how to build a travois and to make a harness from existing tack; to keep expectations reasonable; and the plusses and limitations of driving.

17. the importance of regular progress reviews; why forward movement is a key to success; and why fear is never an option.

NEW HORSE, NEW PARTNER

Either now or at some point in the future, it is likely that you will be partnered with another horse. It might be a short partnership, such as an afternoon trail ride on a friend's mare. Or it could be a longer partnership with a colt you've raised from birth, or a retired gentleman who is now living his last years with your family. Know that the strides you have taken, and the knowledge and confidence you have recently gained, will work for you with all the horses you meet in the future.

As someone who has been in the horse business for many decades, I have had the occasion to meet and work with a lot of horses. Recently I went to look at a horse that a friend was interested in buying, but before I rode the mare, I checked to see if she would respond to my whoa cue from the ground. Even though (or maybe because) this was an older trail horse, she chose to ignore my request.

Now, at some point in her life I am certain someone taught this mare that "whoa" means stop. Whether she had forgotten that long ago, or whether she deliberately ignored me as a test of my abilities doesn't matter. I worked with her for less than five minutes on the ground with a bridle and snaffle bit, as the owner only had an ill-fitting halter and was using a piece of clothesline for a lead. We did walk/whoa transitions with the hand signal, using stern facial expressions, firm voice, rigid body posture, and glares into her eye. Then we did walk/trot/whoa transitions, turns, and backing with the same accompaniment. It didn't take much. Even though the mare had not gone through My Horse, My Partner training, she responded to the confidence I projected as an authority figure. After a few minutes this little mare suddenly "remembered" that she knew what "whoa" meant.

Her recognition of me as her dominant, although temporary, partner extended to the saddle. She performed the best her limited training would allow, having decided that it would be much easier for her in the long run just to do what I asked, rather than fight with me. And had I chosen to ride before making sure she would stop when asked? She might have "tested" me by making a run for the woods, or she could have chosen to take me into a three-sided shed, or just refused to move. Ultimately, the mare turned out to be just as she was represented, a "dead-broke" (if somewhat spoiled) trail horse. She just needed, and wanted, some guidance.

My experience with this mare also exemplifies a huge benefit of these activities: respect. With trust and confidence comes respect. Your equine partner cannot successfully complete any of the My Horse, My Partner activities unless she respects you. Many of the earlier activities are designed specifically to help you earn your partner's respect. But you can earn respect from any horse, now that you understand how horses think, see, and hear—and now that you know how to read the signals a horse is giving you.

Earlier I said that I don't believe in quick fixes. And I don't. But you can use the confidence, body language, facial expressions, voice, and equine understanding with horses who have not gone through the program to help them load into a trailer, receive veterinary care, calm down when stressed, and in many other circumstances. Short term is not the same as a quick fix, but it can get you through a stressful time and deliver you both safely to a point where you can work long term to change attitudes and behaviors forever.

SAME HORSE, NEW PARTNER

My Horse, My Partner activities will also give your equine partner a foundation to use with all humans, and he should prove to be a reliable and steady partner for any human with whom he shares time.

In the world of equine-assisted activities and with school horses, it is possible that dozens of humans will have contact with a specific horse in a single day. The horse must cooperate with each of them, and that is tough for a horse to do, especially because individual people relate to horses in different ways. A horse who has successfully completed all the activities should come to a stop when her leader stops walking. It doesn't matter if the leader is showing confidence, or if she says "whoa," or if she tugs on the halter. When the leader stops, a horse with My Horse, My Partner training should stop as well.

This can be very helpful, especially if you have a novice family member who regularly interacts with your equine partners. A horse who has been through the activities should be respectful to all and do her best to quietly and patiently figure out what is wanted, even when receiving conflicting signals from her human. In that way, the training also provides a level of safety for both horse and human. Being quiet, respectful, and patient is definitely better than bucking, rearing, bolting, biting, or kicking.

AMAZING RESULTS!

Chances are, the experiences you had with these activities and the knowledge they produced are completely different from what you expected—not necessarily better or worse, just different. It is like that for me with every horse. And over the years I realized that like a new friend, I have a perception of who a horse is when I begin working with her. I can see, in Nomo's case, that she is an older dark bay Thoroughbred mare with experiences in motherhood, polo, and dressage. What I didn't see early on was the incredibly nurturing nature, the extreme intelligence, or the strong desire to please. I didn't see those positive qualities because I did not know her.

As you break through the layers and learn more and more about your equine friend, you will discover that the horse you thought you had doesn't really exist. The horse you really have is far more. Who knew a pudgy little Haflinger gelding like Nacho would have such personality, or that he'd have the makings of a dressage horse? Or that laid-back Nelson is actually quite ticklish? Or that Valentino loves cats? It is absolutely amazing what you can discover about your equine friend, what you can learn from her, and how hard she will try to please you, once you understand who and what you are seeing.

Will My Horse, My Partner training deliver to you a perfect, bombproof horse? No. While it will significantly reduce the element of surprise in your partner's life, a new and "potentially life-threatening" object your partner has never seen or heard before is always just around the corner. As with Valentino and the stagecoach, even if your horse is startled, if he has had My Horse, My Partner training, chances are that he will not bolt, spin, or buck. Instead, he will turn to you for guidance. Your horse's "stagecoach incident" may not surface until next month or next year, but the potential for surprise is always there. You can, however, reduce the risk of surprise while exposing the real horse underneath the outer wrappings. That in itself is an amazing experience.

THE NEXT STEPS 18

By now you have realized that every horse is a unique and remarkable individual. Just like people, no two horses have the same personality, thoughts, likes, dislikes, temperament, and quirks.

Once a horse completes the activities, most horses keep My Horse, My Partner training fresh in their minds. But just as a person might need to occasionally glance at a reference or training manual, sometimes a horse will need a quick review of a specific activity. Nacho, Lady, Nelson, and Valentino fall into this category. Once a concept is solidified in each of their minds, it is there forever. A change in location, light, sound, or other variable can temporarily cause these horses to misinterpret a situation, but a calm and patient human partner will quickly redirect these horses toward the correct response.

A few horses, including Nomo and Lucky, need more frequent refresher sessions. For different reasons, the retention level of these horses is not as high. Nomo's protective, mothering nature sometimes lets instinct overtake training, and Lucky's hesitant personality sometimes causes him to second-guess himself.

Horses who in the past have been mistreated, abused, or neglected, and horses who have had terrifying experiences in their life, such as a barn fire, may also need regular maintenance work. Because of their unfortunate history, these horses have more ground to cover in the areas of trust, confidence, and respect. Where most horses are starting at ground zero, these horses are starting at about a minus forty-two. Retention typically is low, but you can still achieve signifi-

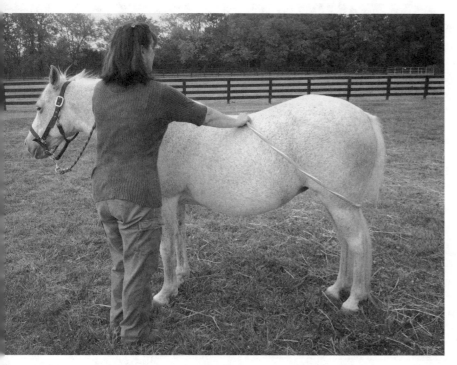

Even the most stable of partners need an occasional review. Reviews can also be helpful to the human partner.

cant results through great patience and absolute consistency.

When all is said and done, these abused, neglected, or traumatized horses may never reach their full potential. Just like a child who has been abused, or an adult who has overcome tremendous odds just to survive, it is sometimes helpful to remember that the fact that they are functional is a miracle in itself. The successes you find with these horses will come in small doses, but in one form or another, there will be success.

Horses aren't the only ones who sometimes need a refresher course. People actually need reminders more often than horses do. CNN recently reported that the average person today processes more information in a single day than the average person in the seventeenth century did in a lifetime! No wonder we have trouble remembering things.

It has taken me a lifetime to develop and refine My Horse, My Partner activities, and I learn more about the process every time I go through it. So don't expect to remember everything the first time through, or even the fifth. It is unreasonable to expect to learn or remember everything the first few times around. When I give clinics, I meet a lot of great people. Many of them tell me that as soon as they finish My Horse, My Partner, they turn right around and go through it again—with the same equine friend. The second time is not necessarily for their partner. It is for themselves.

TUNE-UPS

While it is not necessary to go through all of the activities with your equine friend more than once, it is sometimes helpful to revisit certain areas. Maybe you and your horse have begun a new type of activity, such as barrel racing or eventing, and through that activity you find that your expertise in a specific area needs to be improved. Or, you might begin to see some behavioral issues developing.

So how do you know when a tune-up is in order? Here are a few key signs to look for in your partner.

HE BECOMES PUSHY

Your partner might walk all over you or wiggle too much in the cross-ties, or maybe he ignores your cues when under saddle. These are signs that a "whoa" session is needed. Just go back and revisit that activity from the ground up. Your horse might be testing you, or something may have happened that caused him to question your position as the dominant partner. In either case, he needs to realize that when you say "whoa," his only option is to stop. With this realization comes respect and improved behavior.

SHE REFUSES OR IGNORES CUES

Maybe your horse does not want to load into the trailer, or refuses to walk into the barn or another area. She might also ignore you when you ask her to turn or trot. There are two possible causes: one, she sees or hear something that frightens or confuses her; or two, she is testing her boundaries. But don't worry. Here are several activities that will help.

First analyze the situation thoroughly to determine if there is something she sees or hears that is sending up red flags. Is the trailer new? If so, let her inspect it. Is it dark inside? Maybe she thinks you are asking her to walk into a black hole, so open a side door. Next, determine if the problem happens at a specific location. Does the behavior still occur when you park the trailer on the other side of the driveway, or if you turn it the other direction? How about in the pasture? Think like a horse to find out what it is about that specific thing in that specific spot that is causing her to misbehave.

The second remedy is to go back to leading patterns. This works especially well if she is testing you. Simply set up a challenging course and be insistent that she work hard to get it right. Practice lots of turns, stops, starts, and changes of gaits. This reminder activity lets your partner know that you mean business, so make sure she follows your every direction to the letter. Additionally, as you demand perfection in the maneuvers, it reinforces her respect for you. Once she respects you, the pushy behavior will stop.

If your equine friend develops a new behavior, going back into your toolkit and My Horse, My Partner activities can often turn the conduct into something more positive.

YOUR PARTNER SPOOKS

It is important to determine if the spooking is a one-time event or something that happens more often. If it is an isolated incident and your partner quickly regains focus, do not worry too much about it. We all can be startled occasionally. If, however, it happens often, or if she bolts across the field and ignores you for half a mile, some desensitization activities should be reviewed.

Concentrate on the core category of whatever is spooking her. To correctly determine what that might be, go back to what your horse hears, sees, and feels. Is a shaft of light blinding her? Maybe rounding a corner brings her into an unexpected cold breeze. Look at the world from her perspective. Could she hear an unusual sound from a nearby construction site? Did a friend wearing fluorescent orange muck boots cause her to jump? Decide whether the scary element is based in color, movement, or sound; then go about making a unique event routine through desensitization. Practice, practice, practice. Consistency and routine should take care of it, but the specific desensitization you do to correct this may be something you have to revisit briefly every month—or week—for retention to stick.

You may also need to spend time reinforcing the whoa cue, but know that your horse will not be able to focus on stopping while she is frightened. Usually, once you get your partner to the point where she is no longer startled or frightened, she will stop just fine.

YOUR FRIEND HAS A BAD ATTITUDE

Often a bad attitude is caused by boredom. Another cause is laziness or lack of respect. First try basic leading, longeing, and ground driving exercises, and require your horse to perform well. He has to know there are no other options. Horses not only need boundaries, they crave them. If you are not presenting yourself as a strong partner, your horse can become frustrated and sour.

If that does not help, or if you are sure you are offering a strong and structured foundation for your partner, try introducing a few new toys or games. Just like a kid on a rainy day, your partner can become bored. Challenge his intelligence and invent a new game, or simply put him in a different stall, pasture, or paddock. Introduce him to a new equine friend, or go on a trail ride. If he is a dressage horse, try reining just for a day. If he is a barrel horse, practice showmanship at halter. In short, shake up his life a little. You'd be bored, too, if every day was the same, if you were not being challenged, and if you never learned anything new.

Another possibility is that your horse is in pain or not feeling well. A saddle can cause back soreness, a kick from a herdmate can raise a bruise, and a cold or allergy can make anyone feel sluggish. Internally, an ulcer, a kidney or urinary tract infection, or even dental problems can cause a horse to behave poorly. Be sure to consider each of these possibilities before creating a plan of action.

HE EXHIBITS DANGEROUS BEHAVIOR

Biting, kicking, rearing, and bolting should never be tolerated. You have about three seconds to discipline a horse, or the discipline will not be effective. If you are leading a horse who misbehaves, immediately show the horse your displeasure through use of your voice, eyes, hands, facial expression, and body language. But before it happens again, make an effort to understand why the behavior occurred. Did your gelding act up because his back is sore, or is he a little spoiled? Understanding why dangerous behavior occurs allows you to take steps to prevent it from happening again in the future.

In instances of biting, the rope twirl works wonders; however if the biting is caused by soreness, you need to help his back become strong. Get rid of the soreness and the biting behavior will disappear. You can check for soreness by running your hands firmly over your horse's entire body. Watch his body language as you do this and he will tell you with raised head, pinned ears, or nipping teeth when you hit a sore spot. You can also move his head, shoulders, and legs around watching for the same reactions. If you find soreness, contact your veterinarian, or an equine massage or chiropractic professional, for appropriate treatment. In the meantime, the rope twirl lets your friend know that the behavior is not acceptable.

Did your partner kick because she was threatened by another horse coming too close, or is she lazy and kicking because she is angry that you asked her to trot? Here is another opportunity to bring out your equine thinking cap and figure out what is wrong. If your partner was threatened, just remove the threat. If she is lazy, go back to basic leading to first build up respect, then move to longeing (preferably free longeing), to let her know she has to move when you ask her to.

⊙⊙

Rearing can be caused by fright or frustration or it can be a learned habit that gets a horse out of a day's work. In the case of the latter, you should seek the advice of a professional trainer. In either of the two former cases, you can isolate the problem, then desensitize, although it is probably also best to do so under the guidance of a professional.

⊙⊙

Unless it is part of a spooking issue, bolting is usually caused by a lack of respect. Bolting is not the real issue; your tenuous position as the dominant partner is. After some basic whoa activities, longe your horse with a longe line. If your longeing skills are not strong, practice with a different partner until you are more competent.

Start in a small area, such as a paddock, and insist that your equine friend perform just as you ask. If he does not stop, use a chain for a session or two. When you can longe without a chain in that location, move to a larger one, but be absolutely sure that you have your horse's attention and respect before doing so. Keep moving up in area until he listens to you, without question, in a large, fenced field. While you will be reinforcing the problem, rather than the solution, if your partner gets away from you, never allow yourself be dragged. Your safety is of primary importance.

This is another area where pain or illness could be a contributing factor. Take time to observe your horse when he is on his own. Does he relate to other horses as he normally does? Does he walk, play, lie down, and move about normally. How about food? Does he eat as usual? Are his temperature, pulse, and respiration normal? If the answer to any of these questions is "no," or if you are unsure, please consult your veterinarian.

⊙⊙

There are, obviously many other situations and scenarios, but this gives you a good start for troubleshooting, and some basic ideas for follow-up.

TROUBLESHOOTING YOURSELF

But what about you? You and your equine friend are a team and there are going to be times when he is light years ahead of you. Following are some indications that you could use additional practice.

YOU LACK CONFIDENCE

If you are relatively new to horses, then it is natural that you at times feel insecure. Even if you have been around horses all your life, if you are working in a new discipline or learning new techniques you cannot be confident until you gain more experience with the specific activity.

The trouble lies in the fact that your horse is acutely aware of your uncertainty. If your partner is confident with a specific activity, then he may have enough confidence for you both. Horses can be wonderful teachers. On the other hand, your insecurity may pass on to your partner and cause him to lose faith in you.

To help build confidence, go back to the basics. Decide if there is a specific skill you are not comfortable with, or if it is working with your partner in general that you are not confident about. Either way, go back into your comfort zone and build from there.

If you are comfortable long lining at the walk but not the trot, determine what it is specifically about the trot that you are not comfortable with. Then practice that one thing for very short periods of time. For example, ask your partner to trot eight to ten steps, and then stop. If you repeat, repeat, repeat, over and over again just like you do when your partner is having trouble, you will become more comfortable with the activity.

Find confidence in meeting small challenges. When you can trot ten steps with certainty, go for fifteen, then twenty. Before long, you will be doing just fine.

YOU ARE CONFUSED

Every time you become confused about a process or activity, you pass that feeling along to your equine partner. As it is hard to inspire trust when you are confused, the best thing to do is stop. Take time to work the problem out in your mind before continuing. If you can't, for example, figure out what your partner is telling you, stop. Think. Reason it out. If you have difficulty organizing the longe line with the longe

Preventive Maintenance

Ideally, once you and your partner complete My Horse, My Partner, you will not have to do much in the way of review. You can strengthen the bonds between you and reinforce your shared experiences on a daily basis by doing four simple things.

1. BE CONSISTENT. Every time you discipline your partner, discipline in the same way. Praise the same way every time you give praise. When you give a cue, give it in an identical manner to the last time you gave it. Your horse will thrive on your steadiness and reliability.

2. BE FAIR. Make a genuine effort to understand your horse. Listen to what he is saying. Study him. Get to know everything about him. Make him your new best friend. Do not jump to conclusions about possible bad behavior. Instead, look at the world through his eyes, and then weigh all of the possibilities before setting a course of action. Your partner will thank you for this every day by performing to the very best of his ability.

3. BE PATIENT. If you lose your temper, you will also lose every bit of trust your partner has in you. It is far better to walk away for a few minutes than it is to jeopardize months of work. If you lose your temper, your partner will view that as unstable behavior. He won't know what to expect from you, and will no longer trust that you will behave toward him in a reasonable manner. It can be hard to be patient, but it will be even harder to lose the trust of a friend.

4. BE REPETITIVE. Repeat everything until you both are confident with the activity. It might be five times. It might be five thousand times. Your horse needs this repeated behavior for it to make any kind of sense to her.

We humans communicate so verbally that we have forgotten the many nuances a blink of an eye can produce. Even the flick of an ear can have many different meanings to a horse, depending on the circumstances surrounding it. For better or for worse, repeating our behavior identically over and over again and praising the desired response is the best way to teach our equine friends our language, and to let them know our wishes.

whip, stop. Practice on your own. It is important to be a strong partner to your horse, so back off. When you have figured it out, try again.

YOU ARE IN A BAD MOOD

Sometimes we wake up on the "wrong side of the bed" or events happen that make us wonder why we even bothered to get out of bed. It happens to everyone. You know that spending time around your equine partner can turn your day completely around. However, it is crucial that you know that if you are upset, your horse knows this and can also become upset. For all the many hours you have studied your partner, she has studied you far more. She still knows you much better than you know her.

For that reason, sometimes it is better to do peripheral chores instead of actively working with your friend. Instead of a planned session, take your horse for a walk and use the time to talk out your problems with her. Sit on a fence post and watch her graze. Work your angry energy off by mucking stalls or moving hay bales. You will be doing both yourself and your partner a favor by changing plans and saving any direct work with your friend for another day.

YOU NO LONGER TRUST YOUR PARTNER

It's a frequent scenario: something happens that scares you or causes you to lose trust in your partner. Maybe you fell, or maybe he exhibited unusual behavior that you did not understand. The result is that you no longer have the level of trust in your horse that you once did.

Again, it is important to pinpoint the action that caused the trust issue, and to go back to the steps that preceded it. To do this, think like your partner. Determine why the event happened. Once you know the reason, you can make a course of action. If your horse jumped sideways (and over you) after being frightened by blankets draped along a fence, you know to desensitize with blankets, which will build your partner's confidence in you both. You can also lead your partner along the blanketed fence so often that the unique situation is made routine.

If your horse repeatedly walks all over you he probably does not respect your personal space . . . or you. If this is the case, go back to basic leading and whoa exercises and repeat them over and over until

Lady considers the trust, confidence, and respect she has developed a privilege. She is obviously pleased to be doing what she does best: making her Saddle Up! kids happy.

your horse responds correctly. You may initially need to use a lead chain to get his attention.

In either situation, determine the cause, go back to a comfort level (either your horse's or yours), and rebuild the trust through repetition.

THE FINAL WORD

Horses are amazing beings. They are our friends and partners, our teachers and our students. Our relationships with them can be as complex as any with a spouse, a parent, or a child. But it is up to us to tap into all horses have to offer. You can sit back and enjoy the view, or you can be part of a remarkable ride. I hope you choose the ride. If you do, it will be one you will never forget.

WINDING UP

✿

For additional resources regarding My Horse, My Partner activities, check out my Web site at www.lisawysocky.com. Posted there are additional leading patterns, short articles, ideas from readers, news, photos, and more. If you have questions, please e-mail me at lisa@powerofhorses.com. I will personally answer as many e-mails as possible, and will also list answers to similar questions on the Q&A area of the My Horse, My Partner part of my Web site.

For more information on equine-assisted activities or therapeutic riding opportunities in your area, contact the North American Riding for the Handicapped Association, or go to www.narha.org. These programs are remarkable in so many ways and have the ability to change thousands of lives . . . including yours!

In closing, I wish you all amazing experiences and a lifetime of confidence, respect and trust with your equine friends.

RESOURCES

BOOKS

Dines, Lisa. *Why Horses Do That*. Willow Creek Press, Minocqua, WI: 2003.

Dorrance, Tom. *True Unity: Willing Communication Between Horse and Human*. Give-It-A-Go Enterprises, Bruneau, ID: 1977.

Grandin, Temple and Catherine Johnson. *Animals in Translation: Using the Mysteries of Autism to Decode Animal Behavior*. Scribner, New York, NY: 2005.

Harman, Joyce, DVM, Andy Foster, and Wendy Murdoch. *The Horse's Pain-Free Back and Saddle-Fit Book*. Trafalgar Square: 2005.

Hawcroft, Tim. *A–Z of Horse Diseases and Health Problems*. Ringpress Books, Ltd., Lydney, UK: 1993.

Miller, Robert M., DVM., and Rick Lamb. *The Revolution in Horsemanship and What it Means to Mankind*. The Lyons Press, Guilford, CT: 2005.

Naviaux, James L., DVM. *Horses in Health and Disease*. Lea & Febiger, Philadelphia, PA: 1985.

Roberts, Monty. *The Man Who Listens to Horses*. Random House, New York, NY: 1996.

Williams, Moyra. *Practical Horse Psychology*. Wilshire Book Company, North Hollywood, CA: 1973, 1977.

Wysocky, Lisa. *The Power of Horses*. Fura Books, Minneapolis, MN: 2002; and *The Power of Horses II*, The Lyons Press, Guilford, CT: 2008.

Zeitler-Feicht, Margit. *Horse Behavior Explained: Origins, Treatment, and Prevention of Problems*. Trafalgar Square: 2004.

WEB SITES

www.ansi.okstate.edu/breeds/horses
Extensive listings and descriptions of horse breeds

www.globepequot.com
Click on Special Interests, then Equestrian, for great horse books

www.horsecity.com
Excellent web resource for all things horses

www.horsehavenoftn.com
The organization that rescued Valentino

www.lisawysocky.com
Author's site, with extra leading patterns and other resources

www.narha.org
North American Riding for the Handicapped Association

www.nutrenaworld.com
Click on Knowledge Center for articles on feeding horses

www.saddleupnashville.org
Home of horses featured in My Horse, My Partner

www.spookless.com
Source for CDs of sounds made especially for horses

INDEX

body language and, 47

commands, 39–45, *40*, 61, 71–73

confusion, signs of, 94, 148, 193, 195

discomfort, signs of, 19, 29, 52, 56–57, 63

distress, signs of, 157

greetings, 16–17

hands-on process and, 15–20, 26

play *vs.* frustration, 81

resistance, 74, 94, 115, 116

compact discs (CDs), 9, 103, 104

confidence building

horses and, 58, 144, 179

human partners and, 3, 161, 164, 179, 193

confusion, 94, 148, 193, 195

crowding, 21

desensitization training, overview

benefits of, xiii–xiv

history of, 28

horse's stage of development and, xv

mastery of steps and technique, xvii–xviii, 20, 155

new horses/partners and, 184–86

reasons for, xvi–xvii

refresher courses and preventative maintenance, 52, 187–88, 194

determination, 178

directional changes, 94, 149

disabilities, riders with, xv–xvi, 1–2, 197

discipline, 21, 77, 191

discomfort

emotional, 19, 29, 52, 63

physical, 56–57, 191

responding to, 171–72

distress, 157

dogs, 158

dominance, 74

Dondi (pony), xi, *xii*

The Dressage Game, 82

driving

ground, 150–53, *151, 153, 163,* 163–64

with travois (*see* travois)

driving reins, 6, 146

ears, 39, 49–54, 101–2

Eban (horse), 144

Egg and Spoon, 89

emotions, 20, 22, 177

environments, *24, 25,* 25–26, 128, 129

exercises. *See also* pattern work; playing

ear and poll desensitization, 49–58

hands-on process, 15–20, 22–26

hanging items, 137–41, 156–64

leading, 69–75, 78

one object desensitization, 29–38

toolkit combinations with whips, 63–68, *64,* 68

eye contact, 44, 73, 74

facial expressions, 22, 43, 44, 47

familiarity, 121–22, 124

fight-or-flight mechanisms, xiii

The Flag Game, 82–83

food

hand-feeding, 24, 76

as motivation, 34

nutrition, *18,* 18–19

footwear, 7–8, 23